THE SPIRITUAL PATHWAY

Other books by Barbara Berger:

Fast Food for the Soul
Original title:
The Road to Power
Fast Food for the Soul

———

The Road to Power 2
More Fast Food for the Soul

———

Mental Technology
Software for your hardware

———

Gateway to Grace
Barbara Berger's Guide to User-friendly Meditation

———

Editor of **the Starbrow Series** by Tim Ray

———

For more information about Barbara Berger's books,
see www.beamteam.com

———

THE
SPIRITUAL
PATHWAY

A guide to
the joys of awakening
and soul evolution

BARBARA BERGER

**With drawings
by Barbara Berger**

FINDHORN
Press

British Library Cataloguing-in-Publication Data. A catalogue record for this book is available from the British Library.

Cover and book design by BeamTeam Books

Published in 2003 by:
Findhorn Press Ltd
305a The Park, Findhorn
Forres IV36 3TE
Scotland
Tel 01309 690582
Fax 01309 690036
E-mail: info@findhornpress.com
Web site: www.findhornpress.com

Printed in Denmark by Nørhaven Book, Viborg

ISBN 1-84409-022-1

CONTENTS

PART TWO: MIND MANAGEMENT

THE SPIRITUAL PATHWAY

Foreword

How This Book Was Born

I have been a seeker on the path all my life, but especially since that transformative day when my book "The Road to Power / Fast Food for the Soul" was unexpectedly channeled to me during the summer of 1994. At that time, I was trying to combine a stressful career (as a copywriter), pursue my spiritual studies and growth, and fulfill my obligations as a single parent with three sons. I was so stressed that I finally decided I had to take a break. So I closed down my business for three weeks and told everyone I was going away. But I didn't go anywhere. Instead I took my bike and went up to the forests and beaches north of Copenhagen everyday and walked alone, meditated, prayed, sat under the trees, listened, stayed late on the beaches. After three weeks of peace and silence I was just sitting on the beach late one afternoon when it was like I got knocked on the head and a voice said to me, "Barbara you are going to write this book... so get out your pen and paper and write this down." So I got out my little notebook and listened. Then the voice said, "The title of the book is 'The Road to Power' (later also known as 'Fast Food for the Soul') and the title of chapter one is... and this is what you are going to write about and the title of chapter two is... and this is what it's about..." until the whole book was delivered to me... and then the voice said, "now go home and write it." So I did.

Once I wrote the book, nobody in Denmark where I live would publish it even though I was an established author with many books already published. Then my guidance told me to publish it myself and to give it away. At the same time, I had given the manuscript to Jane Aamund, Denmark's most famous woman author and journalist, who was in the hospital with cancer— hoping it would help and comfort her. She read the manuscript over and over again and when I visited in the hospital, the pages were strewn all over her bed. While she was in hospital, I printed 1,000 copies of the book. When the book was ready, she came out of hospital and wrote a full-page article that appeared on the front page of the Sunday section of Denmark's biggest newspaper "Berlingske Tidende". Suddenly lots of people wanted the book and I began receiving letters and calls from people telling me the book had really changed their lives. The book became a bestseller in Denmark and the rest of Scandinavia and it is now being published all around the world.

Since then, I have continued to develop and hone my "listening" skills and I have learned that guidance is always available to us if we will only "take the time and make the space to go within and feel the grace". So "taking the time" and "making the space" have become an important part of my life and I always try to give myself regular time for meditation and silence in nature. The writings in this book are a collection of the notes and information about the evolution of the soul that came to me during the three-year period 1997-2000. Most of the insights were written down immediately following deep meditation or an extended period of silence in nature when suddenly the information was given or almost "spoken" through and/or to me. This is also why—as you will discover—so many of the sections are written to "you". In most cases, the "you" it is written to is me! My guide or teacher on the other side was speaking directly to me.

You will also discover that there are quite a few drawings in the book. This is because information often comes to me in the form of visual images, which I then try to capture on paper.

Then at the end of 2001, I had a dramatic health scare (which quickly faded back into the nothingness from which it came) and I thought to myself, well if I am going to check out now, I should put my notes together and leave them in proper order so that maybe others can benefit from this information. So I did and these notes became the first section of the book. The second and third sections were written in early 2002 to supplement and support the original material.

To facilitate the presentation of this information, I have divided the material into three sections:

Part 1: Soul Technology. This section contains my original notes, drawings and insights into the evolution of the soul and the spiritual pathway.

Part 2: Mind Management. This is the "how to" section of the book and offers practical advice and techniques to help facilitate the daily application of the information presented in the first section of the book.

Part 3: Peace Technology. This section is an attempt to sketch what I believe the practical application of soul evolution and our spiritual development mean and will mean for our world.

I sincerely hope this information will help you on your way.

Barbara Berger
Copenhagen, June 2003

PART ONE
SOUL TECHNOLOGY

Part One: Soul Technology

Nothing is more exciting than to know you are a soul—that you have a soul, that you are more than just your physical body. This realization opens the vistas to freedom, Eternal Life, and substantial support—no matter who you are, where you are, or what you are doing. So of course this discovery is exhilarating.

Let us explore the possibilities.

The Cosmology

Behind the relative world (i.e. the world of phenomena) is the Absolute. The Absolute is the ONE Unchanging Reality.

This ONE Unchanging Reality—the Absolute—is the Source and Substance of all existence. Humankind has given IT—this ONE Unchanging Reality—many names. Depending on the cultural, spiritual, philosophical, metaphysical or religious background, the Absolute is called the First Cause, God, Brahman, the Field of Pure Potentiality, Consciousness, Pure Being, the Force, the Eternal Now, etc.

Regardless of ITs name, the ONE Absolute behind the changing world of relative phenomena never changes. And IT—the Absolute—is equally present in all the relative phenomena we experience in our "Earthly" lives. (In fact, the Absolute *is* the relative, though we usually fail to see this.) Depending on the level of our consciousness and/or soul development, we are able to access or experience (more or less consciously) varying degrees of the Absolute ONE, i.e., the state of Pure Being.

Consciousness development work—or soul development work—is basically to become more and more aware of the Absolute ONE and to develop the ability to contact and connect with IT at will. Thus as the soul evolves, a being develops the ability to dwell more and more in this state of Pure Being.

All souls seek this experience—at first unconsciously, but then consciously—because it is the nature of our evolution as souls. Each one of us yearns to be a part of something greater, to know that our existence is not an accidental phenomenon, but rather a part of an Eternal Reality that is substantial and unchanging. The first experiences of this unchanging Absolute from which we spring are extremely liberating. They are so liberating because they release us from the mistaken belief that we are just physical bodies, destined to be snuffed out at the end of our short sojourn on Earth.

These experiences are also extremely satisfying because they are so blissful. And because we gradually begin to realize and experience that the Absolute is All Good, i.e., Perfect Love, Perfect Life, Perfect Intelligence, Perfect Support, Perfect Sustenance— Eternal and Immortal—and that this in fact is our true nature. As this realization grows, we experience ourselves more and more as the Free Spirits we in fact are.

We can work consciously to achieve these expanded states of consciousness.

This book describes some of the discoveries I have made while exploring the field of consciousness.

What This Book Isn't

This book is not a book about religion—or about the doctrines, dogmas, rituals, restrictions, ceremonies, rites of various groups that have been organized into churches and denominations. Religion, though originally based on man's eternal quest to understand the meaning of life, has been so misused that its origins have long been covered by a veil or forgotten.

What This Book Is

This book is an exploration of consciousness, of Being, of existence.

This book is about spirituality and the spiritual quest, which is the search to experience the Ultimate Reality behind the world of phenomena.

In this connection, when the word God is used in this book, it is interchangeable and identical to words like the Absolute, the ONE Mind, Pure Being, the First Cause, the Ultimate Reality, etc. All these words are just words or signposts—an attempt to express in language that which in fact cannot be expressed but only experienced. Thus, these words or signposts are only intended to point the reader in the direction of the experience of the Truth of Being that we all seek.

References in this book to Jesus Christ, the Christ consciousness, and the Christ teaching are also another area where misunderstanding can arise. As a realized soul, Jesus Christ was fiercely and totally against dogma and the organized religion of his day—and was one of the most radical and revolutionary teachers that ever walked this Earth. Again, his name and his teaching are often equated with organized religion. This immediately triggers negative associations in the minds of many the very moment his name is mentioned, making it difficult to access the Spiritual Truth of his teaching.

The Technology of the Soul

There is, in truth, a technology of the soul. The evolution of the soul and of consciousness is not a haphazard occurrence, but rather an orderly chain of events that beings can go through if they so desire. But soul evolution is not automatic, i.e., it is not an automatic process like biological evolution. This is because we human beings have Free Will and once we have reached a certain stage of development, we can only progress along the Spiritual Pathway by conscious choice. This is the Order of the Universe. Thus the advance along the Spiritual Pathway, which includes the expansion of consciousness and the pursuit of enlightenment, is a conscious choice.

Soul evolution and the expansion of consciousness are a definite process that can be identified, defined, described and applied. We know this is so because the process has been demonstrated to us by many of the world's great spiritual teachers and Masters. They have shown us, without a shadow of a doubt, that progressing along the Spiritual Pathway is a specific process. And in their teachings, they have systemized this process for us and told us how to do it. In other words, they have described the specific and definite steps we need to take to progress along the pathway— and they tell us in no uncertain terms that if we take these steps, we are certain to get definite results.

This means that if you want to advance along the Spiritual Pathway, you can (and must) take definite and specific steps to move forward. It also means that if you

10

are waiting for enlightenment to just happen to you, you are suffering from a serious misunderstanding as to what the Spiritual Pathway involves. You should not and in fact, cannot "wait" for enlightenment to happen because enlightenment is never an accidental occurrence. Rather enlightenment is the result of a conscious choice, constant study, diligent practice, and the dedicated pursuit of this goal.

So I say to you, if you want to grow spiritually, if you want to progress along the Spiritual Pathway and become a fully conscious, enlightened being, you can and should study this process and pursue this goal— just as diligently as you would study and pursue any other goal or subject you wish to master.

It is my hope that this book will help you along the path because besides being an exploration of the Spiritual Pathway, this book is also a "how to" book that describes many of the specific steps one needs to take to progress along the Spiritual Pathway. (See Part Two: Mind Management for the "how to" section of this book.)

Energetic Signposts

Many of the concepts and ideas in this book are presented more than once. This is because there are many different ways of accessing and exploring the Truth. Each presentation or passage, however, is another facet of the same brilliant diamond. So although some passages may seem repetitive, this continual exploration of what is Truth has its own momentum—a momentum that builds up in consciousness and works far beyond and far deeper than what we consciously are able to apprehend. In addition, it should be kept in mind that

11

what clicks for one individual may be quite different from what clicks for another. It all depends on the level of consciousness and development. In this connection, it should also be remembered that words—all words—are just energetic signposts, which hopefully will point to the next right experience for you.

Also be aware that the words I use carry such a powerful energy charge because they emerge from the yearning and the eternal quest of all beings for Truth and represent the most powerful and transformative spiritual teachings on Earth. Thus the best passages for you will be the ones that bring you closest to the blissful state of Pure Being. Read them over and over again and allow yourself to dive deep into the expanded states of consciousness these passages bring to you.

Words are signposts—signposts to the Truth.
If you're looking for the Truth, without signposts you might get lost.

The Big Mind and the Little Mind

Another concept that needs clarification and explanation is Mind. I often refer to the Absolute—the Presence or Consciousness that is Existence itself—as the ONE Mind. Again, this term is a signpost pointing to the Ultimate Reality, which words cannot express. In this connection, the little mind or the mind of the individual refers to the individual's use of this ONE Mind. Often this "little" mind means our "human personalities", which is the sum total of our everyday thoughts and opinions. In fact there is only one mind—the ONE Mind (the Greater Consciousness)—that we all are using. However, most beings are not yet aware of this.

The experience of the soul or Higher Self really signifies, among other things, the conscious realization and experience that your individual mind is part of and identical to the ONE Mind, and is in fact the ONE Mind.

The Higher Self

The soul of man is often called the Higher Self. The Higher Self is the individualization of the Absolute into you, me and everyone else. The Higher Self is the Divine Prototype behind each being, i.e. the soul. The Higher Self is our True Self, the Eternal, Undying Being—not our physical incarnation on the Earth plane.

"Locking on Target": The Concept

Most of the people who come to our weekly meditation sessions are in the first stages of self-discovery. They have not yet established a clear connection to their souls, i.e., to their Higher Selves. They might be on the verge of connecting to their Higher Selves or just vaguely aware of the phenomenon—or they might be trying to establish this connection because they have heard about it or read about it somewhere.

Connecting to the Higher Self (or one's soul) is a life-changing experience, an expansion of consciousness that is extremely blissful and satisfying. It generally transforms one's life because it radically alters one's understanding of this thing called "Life."

I have developed a technique, an alignment exercise to support this process. I call the technique "locking on target". This exercise is an attempt and a method or technology of connecting to the soul or the Higher Self. The exercise involves the alignment of the body's energy centers and the focus of attention on the Higher Self. I also call the Higher Self other names, for example, the Divine Prototype, the perfect pattern, and the soul. The Higher Self has many different names— again depending on the cultural and spiritual background.

"Locking on Target" is the exercise I developed for connecting to this Greater Self.

Once a person has "Locked on Target" and has learned how to do this consciously and at will, his everyday life—his 3rd dimensional, physical incarnation—can begin to reflect more and more of his or her Divine Prototype or Higher Self. When this happens, there is less of a focus or emphasis on the "personality" and the being becomes more and more a channel for the Divine. As this happens, the person becomes less attached (both emotionally and intellectually) to Earthly events and situations.

Preliminary "Locking on Target"

Preliminary "Locking on Target" is the downward movement or grounding of the Higher Self in the lower vehicle—in the physical incarnation. This alignment is often experienced as a "bringing down of the higher energies". When this grounding process is securely in place or fully implemented, the being has actually built a bridge in consciousness to higher levels of awareness or experience. Thus the next stage of soul development is to begin moving upward (symbolically speaking) across the bridge to a conscious experience of higher levels of consciousness.

During this exercise, a being is building a bridge to the Higher Dimensions and once the bridge is built—the being can then "walk" (symbolically speaking) across it to expanded states of consciousness.

When "Locking on Target", the person focuses on the Higher Self, which is symbolically located at the point of the 8th chakra above the head (usually about 1-2 meters above the head). During the exercise, the person systematically brings down the awareness or energy of the Higher Self to the physical body. Both symbolically and spiritually, the exercise provides access and opens the pathway to the Higher Self.

Sound can be used to further open the pathway. Chanting OM stimulates the chakras and allows the further opening of these energy vortexes to the energy of the Higher Self or soul.

The Diamond Pathway

I call the bridge one is building to higher consciousness the "Diamond Pathway". I perceive each chakra as a diamond that functions as a transmitter or a vortex of energy on the bridge or pathway one is building.

The seven main chakras on the pathway in the physical body are:

The Crown Chakra representing Divine Wisdom or the Christ Consciousness.

The 3rd Eye Chakra representing Divine Sight, True Visioning, the Single Eye.

The Throat Chakra representing Divine Expression, Communication, Manifestation, the Word Made Flesh . ("And the Word was made flesh…" John 1:14)

The Heart Chakra representing Divine Love or the Harmonizing Factor.

The Solar Plexus Chakra representing Divine Power or Action (Activity on the Earth Plane).

The Hara Chakra representing Divine Balance or the Grounding of the Soul in this dimension.

The Root Chakra representing Divine Physicality or Body as Spirit incarnating on Earth in the 3rd dimension.

"Locking on Target": The Exercise

See page 199 (Appendix) for a detailed description of this exercise.

THE DIAMOND PATHWAY

CROWN △   DIVINE WISDOM,
THE CHRIST CONSCIOUSNESS

THIRD EYE △   DIVINE SIGHT,
TRUE VISIONING,
THE SINGLE EYE

THROAT △   DIVINE EXPRESSION,
MANIFESTATION,
THE WORD MADE FLESH

HEART △   DIVINE LOVE,
THE HARMONIZING FACTOR

SOLAR
PLEXUS △   DIVINE POWER
LOVE IN ACTION
ACTIVITY ON THE EARTH PLANE

HARA △   DIVINE BALANCE
GROUNDING IN THIS DIMENSION

ROOT △   DIVINE PHYSICALITY
BODY AS SPIRIT INCARNATING
ON EARTH IN THE 3rd DIMENSION

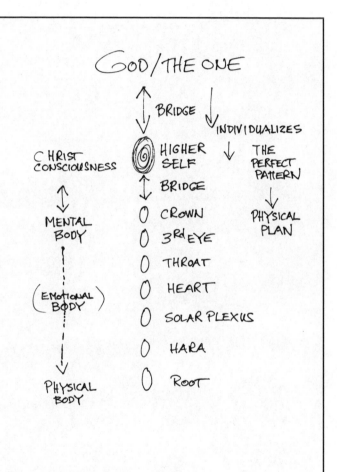

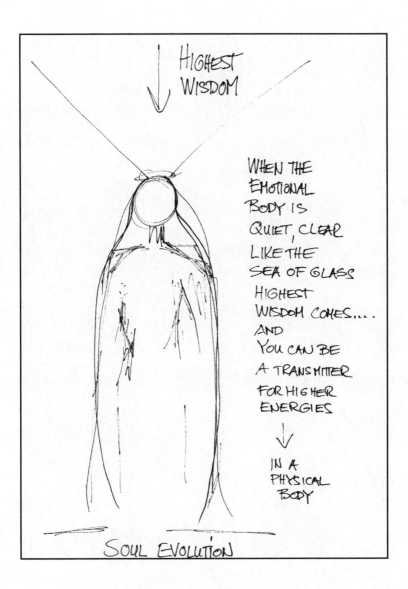

Manifesting the Higher Self

The next stage of development is a conscious and more and more continual awareness and manifestation of the Higher Self or the Divine Prototype in one's everyday life. This happens automatically in the sense that as the being becomes more and more aligned with the Higher Self, he or she will more and more automatically think, speak and act in accord with the Higher Self and the Divine Plan for his or her life and soul evolution.

Beings experience anguish and/or discomfort in their lives to the degree that they are "off target". In other words, to the degree that their lives do not reflect their Higher Selves or the Divine Prototype or Plan for their being. When a being is "Locked on Target", he or she is learning to control the lower self or personality by the Higher Self. When this happens, then the being is connected to the Higher Self and there is a sense of effortless ease and peace in all areas of their lives. "Locking on Target" is the great harmonizing factor.

The Divine Prototype

The Good that each being seeks is the Divine Prototype. No being can ever become less of what they are. They can only become more. This is evolution, i.e., the evolutionary process, the journey of the soul. This is the unfoldment of the Divine Prototype in each being. Unhappiness is a deviation from the Divine Prototype. A focus on the Absolute or God allows the Divine Prototype to unfold.

Anguish and Distress Only at the Lower Levels (Early Stages)

People only experience discomfort, anguish, distress, fear, worry, anger, etc. at the lower (early) stages of development. Once a certain level of soul evolution is achieved, these feelings are no longer experienced. This is because the being then realizes that he or she is an Eternal soul, created and sustained by the Absolute ONE or ONE Mind on a journey of infinite expansion that is always moving towards Greater Good. Once this realization is attained (and this takes place when the alignment or "locking on target" with the Higher Self is secure), a being no longer experiences distress or anguish because he or she views this Earth incarnation in a new light and understands it to be part of a journey of infinite unfoldment. As a result, the person realizes, understands, and knows that in terms of the Absolute, there is nowhere to go and nothing to do. The being also realizes that he or she can never be or become less because evolution is a constant unfoldment that is a never-ending expansion of Good.

As the soul evolves through the different stages, the being or the being's personality becomes more and more soul-infused until the so-called earth personality completely disappears.

Wobbling on the Axis

All experiences of anguish, distress, fear, etc. are a sign that the person is "wobbling on his/her axis", in other words, one is not "Locked on Target". Planet Earth is wobbling on its axis too. Probably a reflection of all the beings on Earth who are wobbling on their axes.

Take a Premise and Stand

"Locking on Target" could also be called taking a premise and standing.

What does this mean? A premise is a foundation thought in Mind. A basic idea upon which one decides to base all one's thinking, choices and daily activities. A good premise could be, for example, "All is Good." This is an excellent premise, one that can only be arrived at after a careful study of the Nature of Reality. Once you have come to the conclusion that *All is Good*, this strong foundation thought will open new doors and lead you on new amazing pathways of discovery. But it is not enough to decide on a premise. Once taken, you must stand firm to your premise. In other words, you must keep to your foundation thought regardless of what you see in the outer world and regardless of what your experience happens to be at the moment. This is one meaning of the mystical phase "Judge not according to the appearance, but judge righteous judgment" (John 7:24). In other words, stick to your premise despite appearances. In this way, your premise becomes your Guiding Light and you are "Locked on Target."

But you say, "What if the outer world is acting otherwise and does not bow down to my premise immediately, how do I know it's not all just my imagination?" Firstly if you are on the spiritual pathway, you must be willing to put this new way of thinking to the test. If these words feel right to you, if they resonate with your own deepest inner knowing, can you not give your wonderful premise a chance and stand by it for 40 days if need be? Then you will have your answer.

Then you will also know that it matters not if it is all your imagination. Because if it is, and you find that by taking a wonderful premise like *All is Good* and focusing exclusively on it as your foundation thought, you can bring forth a glorious life, you would indeed be a fool not to do so. Is this not correct? But you must find this out for yourself. You must discover through trial and error and your own experience of how the universe operates. And if you find that indeed your premise is your Guiding Light, then you will understand why I say only a fool would choose a lesser premise, one that affirms lack, limitation, death and evil, if he knows that by taking the Most High premise of Mind, he can bring forth a beautiful life of unlimited Good and experience the Blessed Realm of Pure Being.

This is why the Masters admonish: *Take a Premise and Stand!*

Conscious Dying

Conscious dying is the ability of a being to move across the bridge in consciousness one has built. In other words, to move to the other side and leave the physical vehicle behind without losing consciousness. When this happens, the soul experiences the "falling away" of the physical body as just that—the falling away of the physical body. This is not Life threatening. Which means that death is not Life threatening. Since we have all passed through the transition called "Death" many times we all know about it. We have all experienced it. Most of us have just forgotten what our souls know.

Since death is not Life threatening, it must be just a scary word for what beings in their forgetfulness or ignorance of the Nature of Reality perceive as a lack of Good. If All is part of the ONE Absolute, if All is a creation of the Absolute, which is the Eternal and Immortal ONE, there can be no lack of Good anywhere in creation.

As we evolve, we will all experience conscious dying.

The Great Master Paramhansa Yogananda demonstrated conscious dying when he left his physical body in Los Angeles, California on March 7, 1952 after concluding a speech at a banquet that was being held in honor of the Ambassador of India. He himself predicted, "I will not die in bed, but with my boots on, speaking of God and India." At the end of his speech he concluded with the words from a poem he had written and then lifted his eyes upwards and entered *mahasamadhi*, which is what advanced yogis call the conscious exit from earth existence. After his passing, his physical body did not decay. According to Harry T. Rowe, Director of the Los Angeles Mortuary, "The absence of any visual signs of decay in the dead body of Paramahansa Yogananda offers the most extraordinary case in our experience... No physical disintegration was visible in his body even twenty days after death... Our astonishment increased as day followed day without bringing any visible change in the body under observation. Yogananda's body was apparently in a phenomenal state of immutability..." [1]

[1] From the introduction to Man's Eternal Quest by Paramahansa Yogananda. A publication of Self-Realization Fellowship, 3880 San Rafael Ave., Los Angeles, CA 90065-3298.

Experiencing Future Incarnations

Once a being has built the bridge in consciousness, it is then possible to go "forward" so to speak and experience the next (future) incarnation or incarnations. This enables the being to bring back so-called "future" energy—or higher energy—into this incarnation. This expansion of consciousness is also another way of explaining and experiencing enlightenment.

When this happens, the being attains the wisdom/insight of the next step in his/her evolution and therefore does not need that lifetime or incarnation. This could indeed be called the fast track forward!

Taking the fast track forward can be experienced on a regular basis by doing the following exercise. I call this exercise—The Next Best Version of You.

The Next Best Version of You

Begin this exercise by grounding the Higher Self as described in the "Locking on Target" exercise on page 198. Once you feel you have connected and grounded your Higher Self, envision the next best version of yourself.

What does this mean? This means that since you are a soul that is continually evolving, each one of your incarnations is part of a progression or evolution to more expanded states of consciousness. Each incarnation is a move up the evolutionary ladder. So this exercise involves focusing your attention on your next incarnation. Since you are evolving from lifetime to lifetime, ask yourself how you will be in your next incarnation. If your next incarnation finds you picking up where you left off at the end of this lifetime, how will you be then? If you move forward from the very

29

best you are capable of being in this lifetime, what will the very best you are capable of being in your next lifetime? In other words, what will the next best version of you be? Can you conceive of yourself as being more evolved than you are now? What is the most evolved you, you can envision? In short, what is the next best version of you? How and who is the most evolved you, you can envision? How does he or she act? What does he or she do? Ask yourself what is the most loving version of you like? What is the most intelligent version of you like? How is the wisest you, you can conceive of? How is the most powerful you, you can imagine? The most beautiful you. The most healthy you. The most enlightened, kind, gentle, considerate, wonderful you. Again what is the next best version of you? Consider all the various aspects of your being and all the possibilities for growth and when you can see, feel, and profoundly experience the next best version of you, then you already are the next version!

This happens because by doing this exercise, you are bringing the energy of the "future you" into this lifetime. So you don't have to experience that lifetime and can skip that incarnation, which is why I call this exercise fast-tracking forward! It allows you to evolve more rapidly because by envisioning and experiencing the next best version of you, you actually become the next best version of you!

Soul Chart

Characteristics

Personality (Awareness focused here)	Soul (Awareness focused here)
Time-based awareness	Timeless awareness
Attached to thoughts, emotions, experiences	Able to witness thoughts, emotions
Affected by emotions	Detached, poised, inner calm
Dualistic (happy/sad)	At all times radiant and free
Physical-emotional-mental bodies	Bridge to Unity consciousness
Belief in a mixture of Good and Evil	Knows All is Good

Beginners on the Path

Beginners on the Path
are moving from
Personality focus → to Soul focus

The shift from a personality focus → to a soul focus
causes confusion because most friendships and
relationships are personality-based and the disciple or
beginner on the Path wants soul-based relationships.

Personality-based relationships	Soul-based relationships
Dualistic, time-based consciousness	Unity consciousness
Belief in mixture of Good and Evil	Knows All is Good
Focus on emotions	Focus on the Divine Prototype

Perception and Reality

Perception:

Human perception and awareness move like this =
From an awareness of the personality → the bridge/the path → to an awareness of the soul

But the reality is in fact like this:
Reality =
Soul → personality → soul

The personality is a creation of the soul. The personality-based being has just forgotten this. Evolution is in fact remembrance. Remembering that the personality is just an aspect of the soul.

When the personality-focused being again becomes conscious of the soul and becomes a soul-infused personality—the lower personality disappears.

The Real You

Suffering comes from identifying with the personality. The Real You is Absolute Bliss, Pure Being.

Thus the mystical phrase: *I AM God-realized except when I'm not.*

THE REAL YOU

SUFFERING COMES FROM
IDENTIFYING WITH THE PERSONALITY

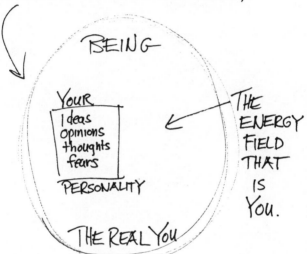

THE REAL YOU IS ABSOLUTE
BLISS, PURE BEING.
YOUR PERSONALITY IS JUST A
SMALL PART OF WHO YOU ARE.

Art and Artistic Endeavor

Up until very recently, Art was personality-based. Now we're moving to Spiritual Art or soul-based Art. They are based on different perspectives:

Personality-based Art	Soul-based Art
Based on the personality perspective	Based on the soul perspective

This shift reflects the awareness or consciousness shift that is going on today. Now we want to consider the same subjects as previously, but from the soul's perspective.

This also explains why most present-day Art (movies, entertainment, literature, art) is so empty and unsatisfactory. Art doesn't give people what they are really looking for.

People want bliss and exaltation. But they don't realize that it is right here, right where they are. And they obviously don't know how to get it.

The Master
Guru
Spiritual Teacher

The Master, Guru and Spiritual Teacher see everything from the soul perspective. That is the difference between the student and the teacher.

Student	Teacher
Personality-based judgment	Soul-based judgment
Dualistic perspective	Unity consciousness
Arjuna	Krishna
Disciples	Jesus
Disciples	Djwhal Khul

The lesser teachers have a combination of soul-based and personality-based judgment. When judgment is sometimes personality-based, they see a mixture of good and evil. When they see only Good, their judgment is soul-based (like New Thought pioneer Emma Curtis Hopkins and the yogi master Yogananda).

The teacher's job is to help the student move from a personality-based focus to a soul-based focus. In other words, to move into unity consciousness.

Shift Your Perspective

Here is a blissful experiment.

Try shifting your perspective from looking at people, events, things from the mortal/ "personality's" point of view to looking at people, events, things from the Soul / Eternal Spirit's point of view.

In other words, try regarding events as if you were Krishna instead of Arjuna or Christ instead of you!

Immediately a great wave of comfort washes over you...

The Nature of Reality

The Manifestation Process

Absolute → Relative
Unity → Dualism
One → Two
Spirit → Form
Good→ Karma

The Soul
The Higher Self
The Divine Prototype

Will Aspect / God →→→ Free Will

All is Love → All is Law (Karma)

LEVELS

GOD REALIZED
THE STATE OF PURE BEING

NATURE OF REALITY = GOD
THE ABSOLUTE

↑

MENTAL/SPIRITUAL

↑

MENTAL LAWS = METAPHYSICS
SCIENCE OF MIND

↑

MIND THEORIES = VISUALIZATIONS,
AFFIRMATIONS

↑

LOWER MENTAL = INTELLECTUAL

↑

HIGHER PHYSICAL = EXERCISE,
FOOD DISCIPLINES

↑

LOWER PHYSICAL
MATERIALISM = FOOD, SEX
MATERIAL SUCCESS

ALL LEVELS IN ALIGNMENT

EVOLUTION

The Nature of Reality
The evolution of souls follows these steps upward:

The Absolute / the Nature of Reality is Good / Pure Being
↑
Discovery of Nature of Reality / Good is a prior / God is Good
↑
Focus on the Higher Self / the Divine Prototype / the soul
↑
Mind Management
↑
Purification of the Mind
↑
Using the mind to create Good / Understanding Mental laws
↑
Discovery of soul / slow release from the "personality"
↑
Recognition of mental forces
↑
Disillusion with the materialistic focus and lifestyle
(breakdown/breakup of old materialistic lifestyle)
↑
Works to strengthen and purify the physical
↑
Works to change the outer order (for example, working for social
change)
↑
Seeks freedom
↑
Rebellion against the human condition and injustice
↑
Sees misuse of power (injustice in the world)
↑
Born—lower desires—focus material world

Human beings can be categorized according to the level they are on. Understanding the level of evolution that a person is on makes it easier to understand the various levels of interest and the focus of his/her attention. It also explains why certain experiences bring distress to certain people and not to others.

Mastering the levels means mastering:
1) Physical technology
2) Mental technology (Mind management)
3) Soul technology

The NATURE OF REALITY IS GOOD

THE HIGHER SELF

Soul ↑

RING-NOT-PASS ———— CLOSED LOOP

LAW IS MECHANICAL

↑ DISCOVER THE NATURE OF REALITY

GOOD IS APRIORI (GOD IS GOOD)

MENTAL LAWS (PURIFICATION OF MIND)

USING MIND TO CREATE GOOD

RECOGNITION OF MENTAL FORCES

BREAK UP OF OLD MATERIALISTIC
    LIFESTYLE

TRYING TO CHANGE THE OUTER
        SOCIAL CHANGE
        PURIFICATION OF THE BODY

REBELLION → SEEKING FREEDOM

SEES MISUSE OF POWER
        INJUSTICE IN THE WORLD

BORN — LOWER DESIRES
        FOCUS ON MATERIAL WORLD

MENTAL

PHYSICAL

↓

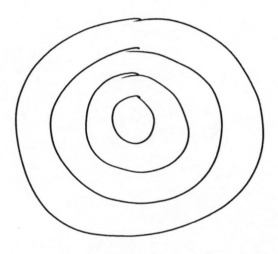

EACH CLOSED LOOP OF REALITY
HAS A RING-NOT-PASS WHICH
REQUIRES AN EXPANSION OF
CONSCIOUSNESS TO GO BEYOND.....
EACH ADVANCE REQUIRES AN
EXTENSION OF THE BRIDGE
USING THE HIGHER CHAKRAS TO
EXPERIENCE AND UNDERSTAND....

The Nature of the Field
From the Unmanifest to the Manifest

Unmanifest
Step 1: The Nature of the Field is Love. This is not an emotion. Love is not an emotion. Love is the givingness of Life. The ultimate support. The Nature of the Field is bliss/pure consciousness. God is Love. Divine Substance. The Absolute.
↓
Step 2: The Field individualizes Itself into all of us. God loves fun, so He gave us Free Will.
↓
Step 3: Intention. Thought comes first.
↓
Step 4: Thought creates feeling. The stronger the thought, the stronger the feeling.
↓
Step 5: Physical manifestation.
Manifest

With God all things are possible because the field contains everything. The field is the Field of Pure Potentiality. That is why nothing (no specific thing or event) is more difficult (harder) to manifest than anything else. This is also why there are no miracles. All things are possible, but the field is governed by Law and the Law cannot be broken. There are no exceptions to this.

All beings are manifesting the working of the Law at all times because whatever they focus their attention or consciousness on, they experience. That is also why nothing outside of us—nothing external—has any power over us or anyone else. (In other words, there are no accidents). The only thing you can experience is what you focus your consciousness on.

Thus the mystical phrase: *You have nothing to deal with but your own thoughts.*

Nothing to Deal with but Your Own Thoughts

Every human being is a focal point in the ONE Mind. Each individual is using the Infinite Mind in his or her own unique way.

And since each human being has his or her own basic beliefs or sponsoring thoughts about the nature of "Life", each being is living in his or her own unique world.

Because thought is creative, each person's Life and Life experiences are self-fulfilling prophecies. In other words, each individual being's world looks exactly like he or she thinks the world should look. Strange as this might sound, it is nevertheless true. No two worlds are the same. Listen to anyone talk and you will discover this is true—beyond a shadow of a doubt.

Quantum physics confirms the fact that we all are a part of one massive field of energy and that all beings and all so-called inanimate objects, are made up of the same energy. In other words, everything—you, me, our houses, our computers, our cars, the food we eat—can be broken down into the same basic units or components called atoms. These atoms can be further broken down into sub-atomic particles, which can be broken down into waves of energy.

At this level of perception, all of creation is one vast field of energy. One vast unified whole. What we experience as Life is what "pops" out of this field *because of* the focus of our attention. The field itself contains all of experience since It is all there is. Thus it is the nature of our attention, which determines the nature of our experience.

This is why *you have nothing to deal with but your own thoughts.* Everything you experience is a result of your thoughts and beliefs and the focus of your attention.

Focus

Focus is the magic wand in this experience we call "Life".

All we have is our focus.

Focus is Who We Are. We are focal points in the ONE Mind, the Mind of God, the field of consciousness.

Our focus is our freedom. It is what makes each being an independent soul. We have been given the gift of Free Will to use this focus in any way we choose.

Self-mastery means learning to control this focus for the Highest Good—nothing more and nothing less.

This also means that everything—all limitation thinking and all forms of limitation—that are manifesting on Planet Earth is an illusion, i.e., a creation of the mind. The only thing sustaining this creation / experience is the focus of the beings on Earth. This is because limitation, i.e. limited manifestation, has no life of its own. Thus when a critical mass of beings change their focus and focus on the Absolute, on the Good, and on Peace, Love, and Harmony—these conditions will automatically

51

manifest. This is because Peace, Love and Harmony were there to begin with. They are *here now* all the time. So they reappear as the illusion of limitation disappears. (They do not have to be created.)

Thus we see that since limitation has no independent existence of its own, there is no power to sustain it. The Good, however, has all the force of the ONE Almighty Absolute behind it. Since the ONE, the Good, is All there is, Good is All-Powerful.

The Magic of Attention

The teacher appears when the student is ready—because the field is the field of all possibilities—Pure Potentiality. So the teacher pops out of the field when you put your attention on it, i.e., when you are ready. This also means:

- health pops out of the field when you put your attention on it
- wealth pops out of the field when you put your attention on it
- love pops out of the field when you put your attention on it
- enlightenment pops out of the field when you put your attention on it
- Pure Being pops out of the field when you put your attention on it
- Etc. (whatever you put your attention on)

This is the Magic of Attention.

Unplugging from the Consensus Reality

It is of urgent importance to unplug from the consensus reality. The consensus reality is the collective consciousness (or you could say the collective "unconsciousness") of humanity—the sum total of the thoughts of all human beings. When you unplug from this consensus reality, all things are possible. This is because the present consensus model of reality translates into limitation, evil, lack, sickness and death—or the dualistic view of Life. To focus on the Absolute automatically requires unplugging from the consensus reality.

For many, to achieve this state will mean fleeing from the cities for a while because in the cities, the consciousness ("unconsciousness") of others confuses. You have no other task but to liberate yourself because in liberating yourself, you help liberate all others.

The Projector in the Field of Pure Potentiality
All beings are creating their reality in the same way as a slide projector projects pictures up on a screen. The projector sends out a beam of light towards a blank screen. As long as there are no slides, all you see is the light on the screen. When you select a slide and place it in the beam of light—between the source of the light and the screen on the wall—you get a picture.

What do you see up on the screen? You see a picture of yourself on the beach when you were five years old with your mother. Then you remove the slide and put in another one—and what do you see? You see yourself getting married when you were 23. Put in another slide and you see yourself old and gray.

You are creating your own reality in the same way—just like a slide projector. And you are doing this on a minute-by-minute, hour-by-hour basis. Just like the slide projector.

The basic building block of this infinite universe is energy or light. And this light or energy—whatever you want to call it—is constantly flowing through the mind of each being. Each being, each mind is the pattern-maker of this light energy. So as this light energy flows through the mind, each being—as the pattern-maker or co-creator—forms this infinite energy into the conditions and circumstances of his or her life and environment. How does this happen? Beings do this with their words and thoughts and emotions. Words and thoughts and emotions are the slides—the patterns—the blueprints—that are put into the light, which is flowing through each mind to create the world—the conditions and circumstances of each person's life and envi-ronment. This includes everything in each individual world including the physical body and health. Words and thoughts and emotions are the blueprint—the pattern, which designates and forms each being's life and circumstances. That is why each being is the pattern-maker of his or her own life.

This is why the experiences and life circumstances of each being are in fact nothing more than their opinion, view, pattern, belief or idea of what this light energy is. It is this individual pattern which is placed in the light that forms the light—limits the light—shapes the light—into the creation, which becomes the life of the individual.

Understanding this mechanism is the key to freedom. With this understanding, it is possible to change one's life conditions and circumstances. This is what it means to be the pattern-maker and co-creator with the Infinite Energy that is flowing through each individual's mind.

Mind in the Field/Mind Is the Field

The Field of Pure Potentiality, which is Infinite Energy, also has Infinite Organizing Power. It is the ONE MIND, the Absolute, the Creator who is the Projector of this Infinite Energy, this Field, which is All of It.

Mind is the First Cause—both the Universal Mind, the ONE Mind—and in your case, the little mind—your individual mind. Or you could say your individual use of the ONE Mind.

As far as you are concerned, nothing exists in your world that you have not thought of. If you do not have the thought, the thing, person, experience does not exist.

Each being lives in his/her own mental world. We experience what is in our consciousness and nothing else. In short, *consciousness is experience.*

Everything man has created was first a thought in someone's mind. Every building, every machine, every discovery, every achievement of civilization as well as every limitation—was a thought first.

Humanity as a race is collectively choosing the reality we are experiencing—whether or not we are conscious of what we are doing. To change the destiny of humanity, we must change our thoughts.

Mind Is All

All individuals are focal points in the ONE Mind. The Mind of the Absolute.

Suffering is attachment to emotions—thoughts—opinions. This attachment to negative emotions and thoughts perpetuates the wheel of negative karma. When beings realize they are part of the ONE Mind—and not their limited thoughts and emotions, they can consciously use mind to choose higher thoughts and emotions such as love, compassion and unity consciousness. (Regardless of what is going on in the outer).

This process of consciously choosing higher thoughts and emotions is often called the process of purification—or the process of self-mastery. Eventually only Good will go out from the person who carefully chooses his/her focus. As a result of this constant focus on the Good, only Good will return. This is one way out of the wheel of karma.

On a higher level, beings need do nothing except identify with the ONE Mind, the I AM Presence—with the Absolute, the Good. This automatically releases the being from karma.

Christ, for example, taught how to use the law of mind and "Practice the Presence" to transcend Karma. That is why Christ is called the Lord of Karma. (See page 170 for an explanation of "Practicing the Presence".) The great Eastern sage Sri Nisargadatta Maharaj taught the same teaching of liberation—how to shortcut karma and arrive at the state of Pure Being here and now.

Karma Is Love

In the larger perspective, karma is love because it is the harmonizing factor in time. In other words, karma is an expression of the Goodness of the Absolute or of God's Love because it is "the bringing of all things into equilibrium". Karma is a time-based factor or experience of existence. Without time and space, there could be no karma.

In this connection, thought is the attention and intention, which organizes the field that is All of Creation. In other words, thought defines the field, creating our experiences. This is also why we say thoughts are things.

When disharmony or storms arise, we could say they are nothing but mistaken thoughts. In truth, they are just different (though perhaps limited) ways of organizing the field. But it is still the same field, which takes on the form of the thought.

No matter what the form, karma—and the passing of time—are the harmonizing factors because they will harmonize the field. The field always harmonizes itself in time and space because the field is always seeking a state of equilibrium. This state of equilibrium is Love or Karma.

Thought Organizes the Field

Thought = attention, intention → organizes, defines the field.

Thoughts are things.

Storm/disharmony = a mistaken thought, a way of organizing the field.

Time and space = harmonizing factors, they harmonize the field.

Harmonizing the field = Love.

The field always harmonizes itself.

The field is always seeking a state of equilibrium.

The Spiral Pattern Is the Visual Image of Karma

The spiral pattern is karma or Love. This is because karma or Love is the harmonizing factor and the spiral is the symbol, picture or visualization of the movement towards the perfect point of balance, the stillness at the center, which must be God, the Absolute, the ONE.

In the spiral movement, energy is rounding itself inwards toward the center. Karma could not be a straight line because that would be a movement in only one direction and karma is the bringing of events and people to a position of balance and harmony. It is only from the limited human perspective that beings perceive events as going in one direction only—in the direction of either so-called good or so-called bad. In the larger perspective, an equal and opposite movement of energy must always occur to create balance and harmony.

This is also why thinking about God, the Absolute, automatically transcends karma. Then the consciousness is automatically at the center point—the point of perfection/balance—the point of no movement—the point of perfect stillness. This state is called God realization, enlightenment, or the Christ consciousness, among other things.

So a galaxy like the Milky Way galaxy is a perfect picture of karma.

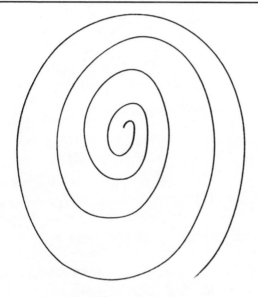

THE SPIRAL MUST BE THE
PERFECT SYMBOL OF GOD,
THE HARMONIZING FACTOR,
THE VISUAL IMAGE / PHYSICAL
MANIFESTATION OF KARMA,
THE LAW OF CAUSE + EFFECT
ALWAYS MOVING BACK UPON
ITSELF TO CREATE PERFECT
HARMONY. THIS IS LOVE.... GOD.

Advanced Teaching: More About the Spiral

The spiral is the visual representation or manifestation of karma in the 3rd dimension. That is why when left to itself, everything is Peace and Harmony.

The spiral is the movement or manifestation of activity or action on this plane. Every action has its equal and opposite manifestation or reaction. Thus, every movement to the left must have a movement to the right. This means the motion of the spiral arises the moment a being thinks or does anything.

This explains why meditation is so important—by ceasing to think or do—all movement will eventually calm down and return to the center, which is Perfect Stillness, Perfect Peace, Harmony, Love.

The galaxies are a visual representation of karma on a much larger (vaster!) scale.

The Earth—wobbling on its axis—is the physical manifestation of the Earth living out its karma—also on a much larger scale. The 26,000-year cycles must be a manifestation (reflection) of this karmic cycle too.

On the personal level, each human being's life on this plane is like the Earth wobbling on its axis as each being works out his or her karma. The Higher Self does not wobble since it is the Divine Prototype— perfect, whole and complete. The Higher Self just sits there—at all times radiant and free—waiting for the lower being, the personality to evolve, discover, become aware of and understand the Nature of Reality. When this happens, the being begins to withdraw from attachment to Earth plane activities and then the karmic wobbling slowly (or quickly) winds down.

The Christ consciousness immediately wipes out the wobbling or karma because it is a total focus on the Divine Prototype, the state of Pure Being, which is the perfect manifestation of unity consciousness. But as long as the being's personality is caught up in the illusion of the Earth plane, the person's life will wobble on its axis just like Planet Earth is. (Planet Earth is just the larger representation of the body of man anyway.)

This is why the chakra meditation—"Locking on Target" and the grounding of the Higher Self in the physical as a conscious awareness exercise—is so powerful. It brings down the realization (awareness) of perfection into the physical manifestation. The more this happens, the quicker the wobbling slows down or stops. Then the realization dawns that All Is Good. All is Perfect Peace and Harmony—and unity consciousness prevails.

Go to the Grace Place

There are three ways to deal with your karma:

1: You can repay your karmic debts. This means you can experience what you caused others to experience.

2. You can turn your karma into your dharma—and do good work / service based on the problems you have had and on the lessons you have learned.

3. You can go to the Grace Place. You can go beyond the mind, rest in the state of Pure Being and/or focus on God, "… the high and lofty One that inhabiteth eternity" (Isaiah 57:15). This is the mystical secret of riding the unicorn's back said the scientist, philosopher and spiritual teacher, Emmet Fox. On that ride problems are not solved, they disappear! This is why Christ is the Lord of Karma.

What Is Will?

"Will" is the self-originating decision to think or do something (for example, move your arm, go to the movies, be happy or sad, focus on Pure Being). "Will" is our ability to make conscious choices. Where does this decision or "Will" come from? How does it arise?

"Will" must be the one independent factor in the universe since it is self-originating. Hence "Will" must be the equivalent of First Cause. Thus we see that the expression of "Will" in human beings is what makes us Godlike since "Will" is a unique characteristic of the Absolute, also called Spirit or God. Hence the mystical phrase about our nature: *Made in the image and likeness of God.* ("… Let us make man in our image, after our likeness…" Genesis 1:26)

This ability to choose our thoughts and direct the focus of our attention by our own volition is what makes us free. The rest of manifest creation, i.e. nature, animals, plants, galaxies, does not have Free Will. These phenomena must therefore be the effects of a cause because without the ability to make self-originating decisions, they can only be the result of some previous cause. Thus we can deduce that all of nature—without Free Will—must be reflecting the patterns set down by the ONE Mind. Since the Absolute is the First Cause, nature must be effect. The Wise say that the behavior of all of nature is animated, sustained and regulated by the patterns in the ONE Mind. I call these patterns the Divine Prototype.

Since we human beings have Free Will and the ability to make self-originating decisions and choices, we are not effect. Rather we are Free Spirit—like God, the Absolute. The Cause.

If we think a little further about the implications of this, we discover that since human beings have Free Will, it must ultimately mean that human beings are not controlled by the cycles of nature such as birth / death—even though at our present stage of evolution we believe this to be so. If we are Free Spirit this cannot, however, be the case. Because Spirit is free and humankind as we have just seen is Spirit. Thus everything that is true about Spirit must be true about us. For example: Spirit is always Spirit. Spirit does not change. Spirit is the cause. Spirit does not go in/out with the cycles of nature. Spirit does not die. Spirit is always free. Unchanging, birthless, deathless, infinite.

The physical body of human beings is, however, an effect. It is matter—a manifestation in the material world. Like nature, the human body is the manifest body of the Divine Prototype for human beings. But because human beings are also Spirit and have Free Will, this Divine Prototype is constantly being influenced by the choices of the individual who is exercising his or her Free Will. So though the individual's thought patterns cannot change the Divine Prototype, they can limit the free, effortless and perfect unfoldment of the Divine Prototype.

This is why the next logical step in our development must be to use our Free Will to drop all limitation thinking, which is just the mistaken use of Free Will. When we use our Free Will to drop limitation thinking and instead align ourselves with the Perfection of the Greater Mind, we allow the perfect manifestation of the Divine Prototype to come forth naturally in our lives. And because the Divine Prototype contains the Perfect Pattern for the functioning of every aspect of our physical bodies, by removing all limitation thinking from our minds, we allow the Divine Prototype to emerge naturally. When this happens, the individual will experience perfect bodily functions without the need for conscious attention to these functions—and will automatically experience perfect health since this is our natural state.

So we see that in the end, each being will discover that the alignment of his/her individual Free Will with the Will of the Greater Mind is the Divine Shortcut to Perfect Health, Perfection on every level, Instant Enlightenment, and the state of Pure Being.

THE PHYSICAL BODY

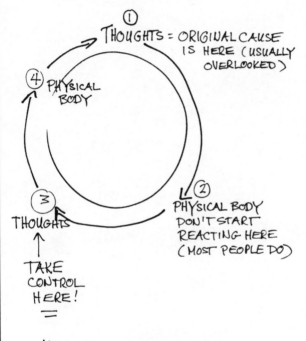

① THOUGHTS = ORIGINAL CAUSE IS HERE (USUALLY OVERLOOKED)

④ PHYSICAL BODY

② PHYSICAL BODY DON'T START REACTING HERE (MOST PEOPLE DO)

③ THOUGHTS

↑ TAKE CONTROL HERE! =

HOLD ON TO THE RIGHT THOUGHT DESPITE PHYSICAL APPEARANCES.

The Physical Body

Do not let yourself be bluffed by the physical body. The physical body is just reacting to your mental and emotional bodies, i.e., to your thoughts and the emotions triggered by these thoughts. In other words, your physical body is not the cause—and never was the cause. It is effect. Your physical body is reacting to your thoughts and emotions, or you could say it is mirroring and reflecting your thoughts and emotions back to you in the most concrete of fashions.

Since this is the case, when you are afraid or get scared because you are feeling ill or bad physically, you are just adding fuel to the fire. You are stimulating the body to continue manifesting disharmony, in other words to go on feeling bad.

To change the situation, you must take control of your mind regardless of what your physical body seems to be doing. (See the section on Mind Management page 147).

Self-mastery means thinking righteous thoughts about who you are and about the Nature of Reality despite outer appearances. The Truth is the Truth regardless of outer appearances and sooner or later the physical body will align itself and vibrate according to thoughts of peace, love, and light. Thus it is of the utmost importance to remember this and to keep reminding oneself that it is not the other way around. So hold to the right thought regardless of the outer picture.

You have nothing to deal with but your own thoughts.

The Truth is True whether you demonstrate it or not.

It is also important to remember: You are Pure Spirit and you were Pure Spirit before you were this body. In fact, the only thing you really want—the only state of mind worth having—is not to notice your physical body. If you do not notice the physical body, if you forget about your physical body—you are free. Then you experience yourself as Free Spirit. The physical body is just a vehicle to experience this dimension with—but it is not who you are. So of course for most beings "dying" or leaving the physical body behind is such a relief. There is a great sense of freedom—and no more pain or attachment to matter or the physical body.

The Bodies

The physical body is the most dense energy. This is the 3rd dimensional focus. But we have other bodies— a mental, emotional, and spiritual body. Each less dense and vibrating at a higher frequency.

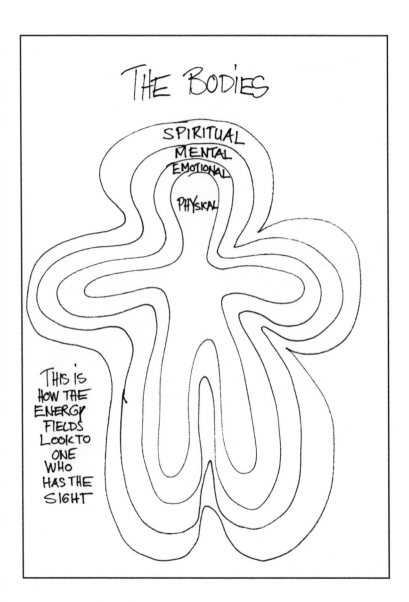

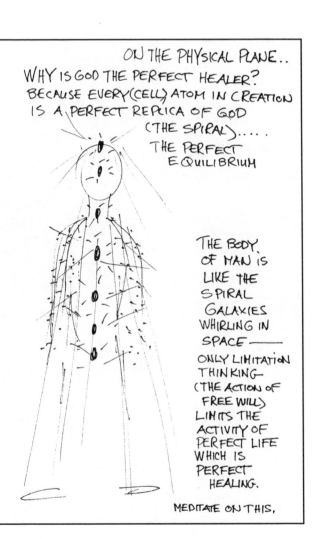

ON THE PHYSICAL PLANE..
WHY IS GOD THE PERFECT HEALER?
BECAUSE EVERY (CELL) ATOM IN CREATION
IS A PERFECT REPLICA OF GOD
            (THE SPIRAL).....
            THE PERFECT
            EQUILIBRIUM

THE BODY
OF MAN IS
LIKE THE
SPIRAL
GALAXIES
WHIRLING IN
SPACE——
ONLY LIMITATION
THINKING—
(THE ACTION OF
FREE WILL)
LIMITS THE
ACTIVITY OF
PERFECT LIFE
WHICH IS
PERFECT
HEALING.

MEDITATE ON THIS,

The Body Electric

Through meditation, focus and practice, it is possible to discover and make contact with the "body electric". When this happens, a human being becomes truly "electrified"—or highly charged. This "body electric" is the radiant light body of a being. (This body of light, i.e., is the "lightbody" spoken of in Ascension literature.) The "body electric" is more subtle than the atomic or sub-atomic body and could be called the body of Divine Substance that I refer to elsewhere as the Divine Prototype.

To contact the "body electric" through meditation, it is necessary to have a clear intention and a razor-sharp focus on its existence. Once a state of deep relaxation and peace is established, shift the focus to the cellular level of the body, in other words envision the cells of the physical body. Then go to the next level—the molecular level, then to the atomic level. At the atomic level, the mind for example can be focused on the fact that each atom in the physical body contains the energy equal to an atomic explosion. Then scan the body and realize that this energy—the unlimited energy of the Divine—is stored within every single atom of the physical body. This realization is often experienced as the sensation of being "electrified" or "highly charged"—an experience that is highly beneficial when the being is experiencing so-called "physical sickness" on the outer plane.

When the electrified sensation is reached, it is beneficial to stay with it for a few moments before ending the meditation.

Or one can continue and direct the attention to even more subtle levels of energy. This being the next level, the sub-atomic level. Continue to focus on more and more subtle levels of energy and on the body of Divine Substance until the point is reached where one becomes aware of the field of Light that one is. This truly is a form of "enlightenment".

Aging and Menopause
In essence, menopause is an illusion, but from an Earth plane point of view, it can be regarded as a shift in level or focus for the being. A shift from the so-called "biological" focus to the so-called "spiritual" focus. In this connection, hot flashes should be seen as energy rising—from the biological-body focus to the head (wisdom) centers.

It is a misconception to think that this transition from a biological focus to a more spiritual focus is a lessening of Good. Since the Absolute, God, is Good and Good is All, there can be no lessening of the Good anywhere at anytime in the Universe.

To most people, the idea of aging is synonymous with the idea of a lessening of the Good. But God—the Absolute—never becomes less. The state of Pure Being never becomes less. It is always *here now* perfect and whole. In other words, God, the Absolute, never sends limitation or a lessening of the Good. But since beings have Free Will, the focus of a being's attention will determine his or her experience. Thus the esoteric phrase: "*According to your faith be it unto you.*" (Matthew 9:29)

The aging thought is a mental pattern or program of bodily decline. This bodily decline thought is often very pronounced in women, but men obviously share these belief patterns too. Among other things, the

78

aging thought results from an attachment to the physical body and a belief that the limited personality is who one is. A shift to a soul focus will allow the being to release himself or herself from these mental patterns and beliefs.

To deal with the aging thought, just watch it when it arises and let it pass by. Then shift your focus to the *here now,* to the state of Pure Being. Think about the Nature of Reality instead. If the mind bounces back and forth, just watch this happen. Be the Silent Witness to your mind's behavior. This is not your identity so just let it go—let the mind do whatever it wants. Then gently return your focus back to the Absolute, to God, the Good. Substitute thoughts of Pure Being or of the "body electric" for the aging thought. Since the "body electric" is your true body and does not age, the more you focus on your true body, i.e., your true nature, the less the so-called aging process will affect your physical body and the more you will become the luminous body of light that you really are. This explains why those beings who focus on the Spirit and on Pure Being—instead of on their physical bodies—become more and more radiant as time passes.

Regardless of what happens in the outer, let it comfort you always to know that the Big Mind (God, the Absolute) does not care about aging and so-called death. The Big Mind does not care about these experiences in the seeming because they are pure illusion—vain imaginings—to the Eternal.

The Way Forward

In this connection, the way forward always involves a shift in focus. A shift in focus from the physical body and the personality to a focus on the soul. A focus on Love and service. A focus on the realm of the Absolute, on God—the Good.

The way forward also means no self-scrutiny. This is especially important if the aging thought is a source of depression or concern. If this is the case, do not indulge in self-scrutiny. Do not contemplate yourself (your body or personality). Do not think about yourself. Do not compare yourself to people who are younger (in the seeming). Stand by your premise that the ONE Absolute is Good. Keep your focus here. Learn to manage your mind (see page 147). Focus your attention on the "body electric". Dwell on the following:

There is nowhere to go—nothing to do.
The Good is fully present here where I am.

Other Good Points to Remember:

The Present Moment Is the Point of Power

All you have is the present moment—the present thought. All you have to heal is the present thought. All you have to do is focus on the present moment.

The future does not exist. (It is just a thought in your mind.)

The past does not exist. (It is just a thought in your mind.)

This is why the present moment is the point of power.

You Are the Cause

The outer world is not the cause. Past events are not the cause. You are the cause. Your present thoughts are what you demonstrate. This means that today is not mortgaged in the sense that today is not the result of what happened yesterday or of outside events. Rather today is unfolding right now because of the way you are thinking right now. That is why all you have to heal is the present thought.

No Accusation

Not only is there nowhere to go and nothing to do, it is important to focus on the fact that each being or form is a Divine creation and has its own integrity. The only task is to focus on this integrity and to do everything in one's power to nurture it and call it forth. This is the true service. This is the true focus on the Good.

Accusation and criticism are heavy burdens to the being who carries these belief patterns. When a being drops accusation and criticism, the Spirit/soul is set free in all its glory.

When there is no accusation, there is nothing to fear.

This is because accusation is the belief that there is something, which is less than perfect Good. In other words, accusation is confidence or belief in limitation. But since the Good is All, we know this is impossible, only a figment of our imagination. Thus if there is no accusation, there can be nothing to be afraid of.

If All is Perfect Good / God, how can one be fearful? What is there to be afraid of?

Without accusation, the yoke of being becomes easy and the world springs forth in all its glory and Perfection.

In this connection, these focal points are good to remember:

Focal Point No. 1
You are Here Now.
Perfect, Whole and Complete.

Focal Point No. 2
Dis-identify from your mind.
Witness your mind.
You are not your mind—nor your vain imaginings.

Focal Point No. 3
You are much more than your mind.
You are Being Itself.

Focal Point No. 4
No accusation = Peace
No criticism = Peace
No judgment = Peace
No opinion = Peace
No resistance = Peace

The Eternal Now

The future is becomes the prison of past conditioning because we allow it to become so. If the present thought is right, there is never any need to worry about the future.

There is no future out there waiting for us → There is only the Eternal Now. The Present Moment is the Point of Power. Future and past do not exist. All you have to do is heal the present thought.

This is easier to do when you know that there is no connection between the event and the emotion.

The Event and the Emotion

Despite what most people think, there is no connection between an event and an emotion. The event and the emotion are two separate phenomena. When a being is able to see the Earth curriculum as a dream—then it is possible to train oneself to always keep the emotion at a high frequency. This is freedom from attachment to people, events, circumstances.

THE EVENT and the EMOTION

EVENT

ANYTHING

EMOTION

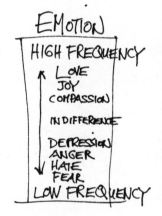

HIGH FREQUENCY

LOVE
JOY
COMPASSION

INDIFFERENCE

DEPRESSION
ANGER
HATE
FEAR

LOW FREQUENCY

The Inner and the Outer

There's no connection (no cause and effect) from the outer to the outer. All cause and effect operates from the inner to the outer.

You do not have to change the outer—or rather you cannot change the outer from the outer. You can only change the outer from the inner. And in fact, you are not changing it. Rather you are replacing it. You are creating something new from the inner—which replaces the old outer picture with a new outer picture. When this happens, beings say the so-called outer has changed. But in fact it hasn't changed—nor have you changed it. You have just projected something new instead which replaced the old "outer".

This is why you should never look at the outer—since it might confuse you and because it has no life of its own. The inner realization is all that is needed. This is reality, more real than what you see in the outer.

The Rock Ceremony (A Meditation)

There is healing power in the consciousness of a Rock.

To experience this *make like a Rock*. When you do, you will discover that the consciousness of a rock is so blissful. This is because rocks are peaceful.

Rock consciousness is closer to the consciousness of an Ascended Master than the consciousness of most human beings. Why? Because a rock has no opinions. A rock has no sense of time or at least a very long sense of time. A rock is grounded. So there is groundedness. Rocks are heavy, peaceful, still.

The consciousness of a rock says, "None of these things move me". A rock doesn't care about the opinions of others. A rock is not concerned. A rock is carefree. Free of cares!

Can you look at your problems from the point of view of a rock? How would a rock deal with this situation? How would a rock deal with this person? A rock would *make like a rock and just sit*. A rock would be unmoved. Try it. This is the rock ceremony, i.e. *to make like a rock*.

The rock ceremony is a good meditation when you are too mental. It has a calming, quieting effect when there is too much random, chaotic mind chatter. Also guidance comes through easier if we do the rock ceremony first. It has a healing power that makes it a good cure for all our ills.

The Ascended Masters also come through easier if we do the rock ceremony first.

THE ROCK CEREMONY

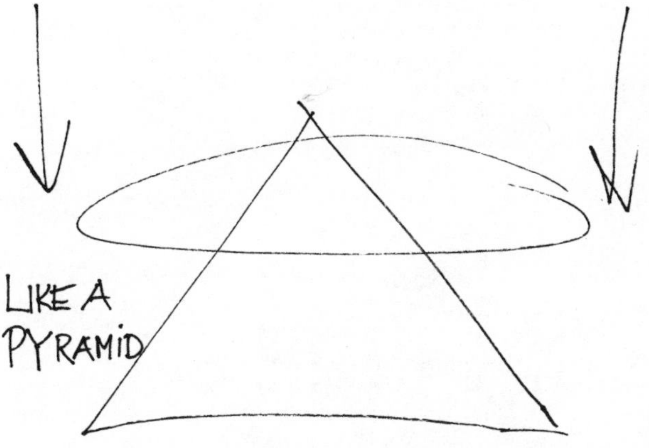

WHAT DO ROCKS DO?

THEY JUST SIT.

Characteristics of Rocks

Rocks don't worry about:
Time
Health
Aging
Opinions
Money

Rocks don't:
Go anywhere
Do anything
Inside a rock is all the Love and Light of God.

Rocks just sit.
The consciousness of a rock is very blissful.
Sit like a rock as the storms rage about you.
In fact, that is all you can really do now.

"Let your aim be true
To the rock in you."

The Separation Thought

Fear is always based on the separation thought. The thought that this is mine—that is yours. The thought that I am this, you are that. That we are different and separate. The cure is the knowledge that the same Love of the Father is in everyone. The Love in me is the same Love that is in you and in everyone else. When beings realize this, they realize that by sending out only Love, only Love can come back to them. This realization is freedom. This realization translates into peace of mind. With this realization, a being can come and go anywhere in the world—without fear—and always be at peace.

Unity Consciousness

When you are in unity consciousness, you understand that everyone is part of the ONE, that everyone comes from the ONE, and that everyone is a perfect manifestation of the ONE, the Absolute. In unity consciousness, everyone is ONE.

Unity consciousness is also synonymous with the Highest Good.

Unity consciousness must be the Highest Good for everyone involved because in unity consciousness there can be no conflict since conflict is not the Highest Good. This means there must be the Perfect Divine Solution in the Greater Mind, in the Absolute, that brings perfect satisfaction to everyone involved.

If we cannot see or conceive of this with our little minds—with our small, limited point of view—the Perfect Divine Solution must exist nevertheless. Otherwise unity consciousness is an illusion.

Allowing the Divine Solution to come forth must be the true meaning of "let Go and let God". Only by surrendering to the Divine Mind and to the Divine Plan can the Perfect Solution come forth since we with our limited perspectives cannot see it or conceive of it. Also if we outline or try to "think out" what the Perfect Solution must be, in truth we are just limiting the activity of the Divine Mind since it is beyond our conception.

Everyone Is Good

Everyone is Good, but most beings don't see this or understand this at their present stage of development. That is why when a being "dies" and leaves the physical body and "gets" this, the soul wants to go back and prove to itself that it can now do it "right". Then the being goes back again and forgets it again.

When a being begins to consciously tread the Spiritual Pathway, he or she finally arrives at the stage where he or she can "get" (comprehend, realize) this information without leaving the physical body. Once this realization is obtained, the challenge is to then live every day with this understanding.

This realization will include seeing all the near people as Good. In other words, to see everyone you share time and space with as Good—Perfect, Whole and Complete—and to experience a deep sense of Love in your heart for every being.

Failure to do so is ignorance, the veils.

Relating to Others

In connection with the realization that everyone is Good, we must often change the sponsoring thought that our closest relationships are the most difficult. The closest relationships are the relationships in the inner circle—with parents, partners and children. Often difficulties arise in the inner circle because we have a tendency to focus on and identify with the "personality" when interacting with people who are close to us (the inner circle). When dealing with people we don't know, it is easier to focus on the "soul", the "higher self" because we do not know their "personalities".

Also we tend to forget to speak the Word of Good—the Word of the Omnipresence of Good—for the people in the closest circle even though we may do so for the others, for example when praying for peace. This we must remedy in our relationships and dealings with people in the inner circle and "judge not according to the appearance, but judge righteous judgment" (John 7:24). And then be totally unattached to the consequences. If we understand that God is Good and God is All, this is not difficult to do.

All is Light!

RELATING TO OTHERS

PEOPLE IN GENERAL

COLLEAGUES

CUSTOMERS

You

CLOSE RELATIONS

FRIENDS

BUSINESS ACQUAINTANCES

THE WORLD

THE FURTHER AWAY PEOPLE ARE, THE EASIER IT IS TO RELATE TO THEIR SOULS....

Letting Go

Let go of the idea that it is important to convince other people of the validity of the Spiritual Pathway—or of the validity of God, the Absolute. In truth, the thought is ridiculous. Each being is only responsible for his/her own God realization. No being is responsible for saving:

- Parents
- Children
- Or anyone else

In fact, this is an arrogant thought because everyone is already perfect and whole and perfectly capable of working out his or her own destiny. This realization allows each being to be free—free to speak his/her own truth, focus on God in all situations, and press forward—and not consider anything but God, the Absolute, the state of Pure Being.

It is also arrogant to feel responsible for other beings because it would be totally unfair to rob any being of the joy of discovery that each one of us experiences as we walk the Spiritual Pathway.

The Good

The Good is the only real independent power in the universe because it is God. This means that evil or disease has no life of its own. It is not person, place or thing. This also means it is only your focus on these experiences that brings them into existence and that maintains their appearance. When the focus of beings is not on evil or disease, they must disappear since there is nothing to sustain them. Whereas when the focus is on GOD/Good, all the Power of the entire universe is behind this focus. This is because you don't have to create Good because it already exists and is already *here now*. You just have to focus on it and let it manifest in your life.

God/Good has a Life of its own—independent of the thoughts or opinions of beings. Opinions do not affect GOD/the GOOD in anyway. This is why It—GOD, the Good—is always there, waiting for beings to discover It. See parable of the Prodigal Son (Luke 15).

All Good—any Good you can imagine (conceive of) already exists in God otherwise it would be impossible to imagine. So all you have to do is focus on it to bring it into existence.

- Perfect Health
- Everlasting Life / Everlasting Youthfulness
- Inexhaustible Vitality
- Peace of Mind / Perfect Peace
- Unspeakable Beauty
- Abundance / Prosperity / Wealth / Success
- Joy / Exaltation / Fun
- Love / Perfect Support / Understanding
- Perfect Home / Safety / Comfort

Focus is the magic wand in God's universe.

Peace of Mind

Peace of mind is the one thing that really matters.

Do you need sleep? No, you don't need sleep—you need peace of mind.

You can tame the mind through practice and meditation. You can train yourself to see with the Single Eye.

You can just as easily be tossed around by success as by difficulties. Being affected by either is a sign of being attached to the world of phenomena. The Single Eye is always to God, the Absolute, the Most High Good, regardless of what is happening in the Outer. Be it success or difficulties.

Take a premise and stand by it. This is the shortcut to peace of mind.

This is also the key to reaching the state of Pure Being—the permanent state of Bliss, Love and Peace that everyone seeks.

True Peace of Mind comes when we are not dependent on anyone—or anything. We are dependent only on God, the Good.

Peace Is Your Nature (A Meditation)

Sit comfortably, close your eyes and breathe deeply. As in all forms of meditation, begin by withdrawing your attention from the external world and focusing on being *here now*. Let go of all the thoughts of the day and just be *here now*. If any thoughts enter your mind, just release them gently and return your focus to the *here now*.

Give yourself time to become aware of yourself, of the Presence of yourself, of yourself being *here now*. A good way to increase this awareness is to focus on your breathing. Just watch your breath going in and out. In and out. As you do this, you will experience yourself slowing down and becoming more and more centered, and more present in the *here now*.

Continue this focus on your breathing for a few moments or minutes. And if your mind starts to wander, just gently return your focus to your breathing.

Now as you feel yourself becoming more and more calm, gently focus your attention on the *silence* that is surrounding you. Whatever sounds you become aware of, in the room or outside the room, focus your attention not on the sounds, but on the *silence* that is surrounding these sounds—and on the silence that is *in between* these sounds. Once you focus your attention on the *silence* that is behind sound and which is supporting sound you will discover that this *silence* was there all along and that it is a vast, huge ocean. Far vaster and far more immense than the intermittent and changing sounds themselves.

When you make this discovery, you understand that this *silence* has always been there, surrounding everything, supporting everything. That it was there before you were born—that it was there from the very beginning—and that it will be there after you leave this body.

This discovery/realization brings an immediate and immense sense of Deep Peace. A Peace that is so huge, so vast, so eternal, so blissful, so enduring, so comforting, and so utterly lovely that you wonder how you could have overlooked it so long!

Finding this Peace is as easy as falling off a log. It takes no effort whatsoever. All you have to do is focus on it and surrender...

Then to your great and eternal delight, yet another sublime realization comes to you: You didn't have to create Peace either. Blissfully, you realize that *Peace* like *silence* was there all along. That Peace—Deep Peace—is always there, always *here now*, and always was. In truth, peace—deep peace—is the Nature of Reality. It dwells in the *here now*, in the vast, immense and blissful *silence* that is the womb of all phenomena.

The state of blissfulness that can be attained by focusing on the *silence* behind, between, above and below can also be reached by focusing on another emptiness: *Space*.

All of manifest creation is suspended *in space*. That you know. But what about when you look inward? When you focus your attention inward—on your inner physicality? When you do, you discover that your body is made up of cells that are made up of molecules that are made up of atoms that are made up of protons, electrons, and neutrons that are made up of sub-atomic particles that are made up of.... And you discover something more—the further inward you go, the vaster the *space* is in between these atomic and sub-atomic particles. This *space* within you is so immense that you discover that most of you is *space— inner space*—the *space* behind and between the physicality of you, which is supporting you. *Space,* which is a vast huge ocean of what—of emptiness, of Bliss, of Peace, of Serenity.

Do not ask what in fact this *space* is because you have come to one of the foundation stones at the heart of manifest creation. *Space* is. It's as simple as that. Just as *silence* is.

No one can explain more or tell you why.

But one thing is for sure—contacting these states in their essence brings to every being that extraordinary sense of Deep Peace that is at the very heart of creation.

And it's as easy as falling off a log.

That is, my friend, if it is your intention.

So now you know.

What it is. Where it is.

But never the how of it—nor the why of it.

Only that it is like a vast, vast ocean of infinite depth—and that this ocean is You.

Such is the truth of it.

You are this vast, vast ocean of infinite depth.

But then you say but what of the *thought waves* that thrash about on the surface of this vast, vast ocean? What of them answer the Wise. But these *thought waves* are stormy, changing, sometimes even violent you say. And what of it reply the Wise. No *thought wave* no matter how violent has the power to touch or influence in any way the vast ocean below the waves that is the real You.

Such is the Nature of You.

Such it has been for all eternity—and such it will continue to be.

This depth and vastness no *thought wave* can touch.

Such is the Nature of You.

So just allow yourself to be it… to swim in it say the Wise.

Because in the depths of this vastness that is You, there is Peace—a Peace that never was or ever will be touched by the changing, restless *thought waves* that come and go on the surface of your mind all day long.

So say the Wise, now you know.

Now without a shadow of a doubt, you know that nothing—not even the most powerful *thought wave* can influence the Peace, which is your Nature.

So you can breathe more easily now my friend and allow yourself to fall even more deeply into this vast, vast ocean of Pure Being, which is who You are and which is Peace.

Thus say the Wise, Peace is your Nature.

This indeed is comforting to know.

God's Will for You/Me Is Good

Since God, the Absolute, the ONE is Perfect Good, the unchanging principle of Perfect Good, His Will for us must be Perfect Good and nothing less than Perfect Good. That means the Most High Good—and nothing less. Now the Most High Good is the very best we can conceive and an infinity of more. This is a pretty amazing thought. Often people think the Will of God for them must be pain and suffering—and that if they surrender to God, their lives will be difficult. But if God's Will for you is the Most High Good it means you are surrendering to wonder upon wonder, miracle upon miracle. You are surrendering to your heart's desire. The fulfillment of all your dreams and an infinity of more. Perfect Love. Perfect Peace. Infinite Joy. Everlasting Life. Inexhaustible Vitality. Infinite Abundance. Radiant Health. Unconditional Support. Unconditional Love.

This is why the Christ consciousness is easy. It's your natural state—to be at Perfect Peace in the Everlasting Arms of the Father. And this must be why Jesus said, "Come unto me, all ye that labor and are heavy laden, for my yoke is easy and my burden is light."

If this is our natural state, if Spirit is fearless and free, then it is more difficult to fear and see separation than to see our natural state of perfection. Since Spirit is deathless, birthless, has no physical body or limitation of any kind, is perfectly free, what does Spirit have to fear? Fear is always based on the thought of limitation of some kind. A limitation of life, a lessening of life, etc. But Spirit doesn't fear any of this because to Spirit it is just an illusion, a vain imagining. Spirit is carefree.

Or as Mylos Melchezidek said: "Look above the pyramid and straight up into space. Then take back the vision—the seed in your heart—of Eternity. It is not cold and lonely but more loving and compassionate than anything you can imagine. Don't look without, but within—until you forget who you thought you were."

If There Is Conflict

If there is a conflict, it cannot in truth be real. This is because the Omnipresent Intelligence behind all of creation would not create conflict. Why not? Because conflict is simply not intelligent! It's as simple as that. No Omnipotent, Omniscient Power—no Power that is Absolute Good—would create a universe or in fact any situation that is less than the Most High Good, i.e. a situation in which there is so-called "conflict" or disharmony. Only a lesser intelligence could conceive of (envision and manifest) what we call "conflict".

If you will consider this idea for a moment in terms of any problem or conflict you are experiencing with another person (for example with your partner), you must arrive at the conclusion that the Perfect Solution (the Divine Plan) for you and the other person must already exist, must be pre-existent in the mind of God. This has to be so because God is All and God is Good. In other words, there is nothing in existence but this ONE Absolute Power that is Omnipotent Good. Thus we arrive at the inevitable conclusion that the Omnipotent, Omniscient Intelligence behind all of creation must have a plan for each of us. And this plan—the Divine Plan—must bring perfect satisfaction to everyone involved in the situation if it is the perfect solution, the Divine Solution. Otherwise it cannot be the perfect solution. If one of the parties in any situation experiences a lessening of Good when resolving a so-called conflict situation, the solution cannot be the Divine Plan. Only the Divine Plan—God's Will for you, me and everyone else—can bring perfect satisfaction to each of us. (Of course we, with our limited perspective, may not be able to immediately see and understand that the Divine Plan brings perfect satisfaction, but this must nevertheless be the case.)

Thus the mystical phrases: *Let Go and Let God.* Or *Thy Will Be Done.*

By surrendering to the Will of Omnipotent Intelligence (God), we are surrendering to the Most High Good—rather than to something disagreeable.

When the Divine Solution (the Divine Plan) emerges (and it emerges when we turn our focus away from limitation thinking and contemplate "...the high and lofty One that inhabiteth eternity" Isaiah 57:15), it will bring perfect happiness and complete satisfaction to everyone involved. If any of the beings involved in a situation are less than completely and perfectly happy and satisfied, the resolution cannot be the Divine Solution.

The Healing Power of the Keynote

To find and touch the keynote of anyone's life will release the healing power within. The keynote is the tone (the sound, the melody, the vibrational frequency) that brings that fine blessed wind from afar—of inspiration—and of the Highest Good.

The keynote is whatever makes you feel most alive in your life—the closest to God—to your Good. Your keynote could be a job, a person, a passion, a talent, a calling, a vision, a way of being, a place. Whatever it is, only you can know it and find it.

Your keynote is your Healing Note. Stick to your keynote. Your keynote will bring you through. You keynote is your connection with God.

The Great Love

That very Great Love—the urge to Love—is in all beings. It is the great misunderstanding of the race to think it has to be directed at one person. The Love was there before the Beloved (the One Person) appears (arrived). The Love is who I AM, what we are... only we have inhibited the flow out of ignorance. Love is not dependent on the Love object. The Love preexists it. The Love was there before. This realization (and feeling), the out-flowing of Love, the Divine Urge, is Bliss—God realization, your natural state, the state of Pure Being.

Not having a "love object", i.e. a boyfriend or girlfriend, can free one to look at the nature of Love itself. This can be a very liberating experience. To discover that the Greatest Love is within.

Love Is Kind (A Meditation)

One of the most effective and wonderful ways to heal all your problems—whether they be relationship problems, health problems or financial problems—is to mediate on and contemplate Love. Meditating on Love is also a wonderful shortcut to experiencing the bliss of Pure Being.

Here is one suggestion of what to do:

Decide to dedicate 15-20 minutes to thinking about, contemplating and meditating on Love. Go somewhere where you can be alone and quiet and then just relax for a few moments. Close your eyes and then systemically turn over some of the following ideas in your mind. For example, what is Love, what does Love mean, what does Love do, how does Love feel, where does Love come from, what does Love look like, how does Love act, why is there Love?

To contemplate Love deeply and profoundly, it is wise to first read and ponder the thoughts of one of the Great Masters on Love. The thoughts of the Great Ones and their words and descriptions of Love are wonderful signposts that can trigger the ever-deepening realization of the miracle of Love in each of us.

For example the wonderful words of 1 Corinthians, Chapter 13 that so many of us know are an excellent way to start a meditation on Love is Kind. "...Love suffereth long, *and* is kind: love envieth not: love vaunteth not itself, is not puffed up, doth not behave itself unseemly, seeketh not her own, is not easily provoked, thinketh no evil; Rejoiceth not in iniquity, but rejoiceth in truth; Beareth all things, believeth all things, hopeth all things, endureth all things, Love never faileth…" Or read the wise words of the Dalai Lama on compassion… or any other text, which helps you to profoundly connect to the energy field of Love.

Once you get a strong sense of Love in your heart and feel its magic working in and through you, you can end your meditation by sending this energy out like healing balm into the various areas of your life. For example, let the healing balm of Love descend and caress your loved one and closest relationships. See how this divine energy softens, soothes and heals all troubles and banishes all dismay. Send Love to your friends, to your workplace, to your distant relatives, to your business associates, and to other so-called trouble spots on Earth. Each time you send this energy out to someone, you will feel how the miracle of Love is acting as a softening agent, immediately melting hardness, anger, criticism and despair. Always this Love energy brings a feeling of kindness to every situation and a renewed sense of hope. This is because *Love is kind*.

Allow yourself once again to contemplate what *Love is kind* means and feels like in all the areas of your life. There is no more effective healing than this. Even in terms of your physical body. Send the kindness of Love to any area of your body where there is distress or pain and let the kindness of Love do its healing work in you. If you contemplate the depths and wonders of Love on a regular basis, there will be no end to the wonders you will experience. Because indeed…

Love is kind.

This is the blessing of Love.

Liquid Light

What would you do if I gave you a Liquid Light Zapper?

An object that looked like some high-tech space gun or long light saber like in Star Wars—and I told you it was your very own Liquid Light creator. And that with this Liquid Light Zapper, you could spray Liquid Light into the field around you and this Liquid Light would become whatever manifestation you decided it should become.

Of course I know you'd look at me like I'd seen one too many Star Wars movies, but just bear with me a moment and accept my premise. OK? So now I've given you your Liquid Light Zapper and I am explaining to you that you can point your Zapper in any direction, press the trigger and ZAP! Out comes this fabulous, radiant spray of Liquid Light and instantaneously it forms itself into the shape, form, feeling, manifestation you think it should have. It asks no questions, your Zapper. It's your Obedient Servant, following your every command blindly.

Well that's a good one, you say to me.

Yes, it is, isn't it? I reply.

Why don't you give it a try, I say.

And trying to humor me, you say OK.

Spray yourself a situation, I say.

Like what, you say.

Anything you want, I say.

Still trying to humor me, you conjure up this scene, which you think is funny, of yourself as a tired, old, grumpy man sitting on a park bench feeding the pigeons in some rundown park in some rundown city and I say why that?

111

And you say, oh it was just a joke.

And I say, your Liquid Light Zapper doesn't have a sense of humor and you say well you do. And I say don't be so sure of that.

So now you understand. Whatever form manifestation you command becomes your reality. In other words, you just point your Liquid Light Zapper in any direction and create whatever you want. And it's not a dream or some Hollywood fantasy. It just happens to be the way the universe works. Which is also to say that until you spray Liquid Light in the direction you're looking at—with the form you desire—there's nothing but a field of potential—the Field of Pure Potentiality, which is waiting to become any reality you decide to create.

When you understand that this is the Nature of Reality what should you do? You should:

1) Purify your thoughts.
2) See reality as Liquid Light.
3) Realize reality is Liquid Light. Understand that this is the key to healing miracles.
4) Know you can direct this Liquid Light easily and effortlessly.
5) Direct this Liquid Light to the Highest Good.
6) Direct this Liquid Light for the Highest Good.
7) Know there is no opposing force.

Since all is Liquid Light and there is no opposing force, this means you are the Master. This means you can direct Liquid Light easily and effortlessly. This might sound amazing, but it is true nevertheless. God made reality so.

What would happen if you started viewing the world not as solid fact, but as Liquid Light?

The Jesus Christ Method

Jesus was a Master of Liquid Light. He did not doubt his ability to manifest. He understood the Nature of Reality and knew he had a Liquid Light Zapper that was always at his command.

He understood that *thoughts are things and things are thoughts*.

His so-called "miracle" method involved three steps:

1. Recognition—He gave thanks in advance because he understood the Nature of Reality.

2. Unification—He knew that things would work out according to law with mathematical precision. Thus he said "*I know that thou hearest me always...*" (John 11:42)

3. Command—He commanded and did not doubt. Thus he could say with absolute certainty *Lazarus come forth*! (John 11:43)

Consciousness Surgery

Consciousness surgery means to remove the error thought. Just cut it away.

This is what Jesus did. He just cut away the error thoughts and said: "...go, and sin no more." (John 8:11)

Once he performed his operation, he said, "According to your faith be it unto you." (Matthew 9:29)

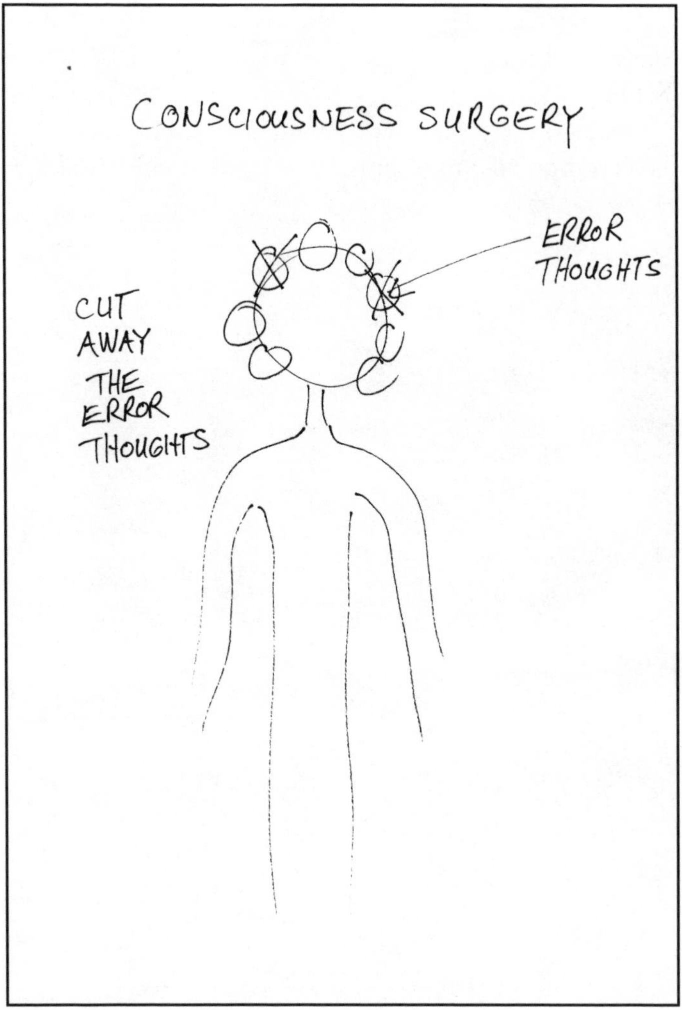
CONSCIOUSNESS SURGERY
ERROR THOUGHTS
CUT AWAY THE ERROR THOUGHTS

According to Your Faith

According to your faith be it unto you. When Jesus said this, he was demonstrating his understanding of the technology of the universe. This statement of the Nature of Reality is true for everyone, no matter what they believe. There are no exceptions to this rule. This is because every being's life is a perfect reflection of his or her beliefs about the Nature of Reality. Regardless of whether the being is aware of or can understand this or not, the Law is still the Law.

The technology of ascension, for example, also holds true for everyone. There are no exceptions to Cosmic Law.

Love and Law

Jesus showed us how to use the Law (the Law of Cause and Effect) to gain our freedom—use it with Love. That is why Love is the fulfillment of the Law!

Without Love, the Law is just the Law of Cause and Effect. It is mechanical and people have no way to steer their course to happiness…. But Jesus showed us the way out of endless bashing (karma)—*use the Law with Love!*

This is the brilliance of his teaching. Without this understanding, the law is just mechanical and you could use it for your own benefit, but until you see the unity of man—LOVE—and ask for the Highest Good for All—you will never be liberated. It's just not possible because asking selfishly only leads to more bashing.

That is why the Christ teaching is twofold—Love and Law.

Law alone—without Love—will only get you in trouble. So you need a Guiding Light, a compass, a lodestone—and that's Love! So Love is the fulfilling of the Law and the only way to make it come out right—for yourself and for everyone else!

This is also why Love is the most important thing of all because even if you don't know about the Law, if you have Love it will come out right anyway.

Thus the mystical phrase: *Only Love goes out from me and only Love returns…*

The Same Mind

There is only ONE Mind.

This means that you and I actually *do* have the Christ consciousness since you and I are using the same mind as Christ Jesus used even though we might not be aware of it. Regardless of our level of awareness, the ONE Mind still must be our mind because there is no other mind! This must mean that if our demonstration is less than the Jesus Christ demonstration, all we have to do is use the ONE Mind in the same way as Christ Jesus used it. He did in fact say this. (Pretty wild thought!)

If the metaphysical conclusions of the world's greatest thinkers are true, this must be the case. Thus if our demonstration is less than Christ Jesus', we can only ask ourselves why we are using the ONE mind in such a limited way—and why we are not making use of our full potential?

If we really get the realization, how will we then use the ONE mind?

Ascension Technology

Ascension is the teaching and technology of the dimensions.

In our case, we are experiencing existence in the 3rd dimension.

It is possible to access the technology of how the soul manifests in the 3rd dimension. To do this, study sacred geometry, "The Keys of Enoch", the mystical teachings.

The Silver Cord is the link between the soul and the physical vehicle.

The consciousness, i.e., the knowing self, only uses the physical senses to know this dimension—to experience this dimension. It is misleading to identify with the body. The soul creates the body—not vice versa. The soul precedes the body.

Question: Why take the physical body to the higher dimensions?

Answer: Taking the physical body into the higher dimensions is not specifically a goal in itself. Soul alignment / God realization / purification / Pure Being is the goal. When this happens, ascension is automatically possible.

Where is all this happening? Where is everything happening? The 3rd dimensional experience is happening in the Greater Mind, in the ONE Mind, the mind of the Absolute.

A being cannot, however, go to the 5th dimension until he/she understands the Nature of Reality and how the Law works. When this happens, the soul becomes the conscious master and achieves self-mastery. Until this happens, souls go to the 4th dimension to rest and then return to the 3rd dimension to continue their learning process until they achieve self-mastery. When they have, they can move on, i.e. ascend.

A being can go to the 5th dimension from the 3rd dimension or from the 4th dimension. It is the same. This 3rd dimensional physicality is only a toy—a tool—a manifestation chamber to learn that thoughts are things.

New Models for Living / Light Work

As long as human beings use their Free Will to choose lesser models, lesser manifestations will manifest. It's all Light anyway. You could say Eric Klein, author of "The Crystal Stair", is right when he says that the Light has been misqualified due to principle or law. According to law, the collective consciousness can keep recycling the same thought patterns, programs, etc. Or use Free Will—and work the law or principle—to send out new thoughts, which will inevitably create new manifestations. Without teachings and teachers, beings will continue to choose limitation because that's all the new souls are exposed to. The teacher / teachings demonstrate that other choices are possible. The teacher / teachings provide inspiration. This is Light Work. Showing that other patterns, programs are available and possible. Inspiring others to choose again.

Without teachers, where would we be?

LIGHT WORK

LIGHT WORK → ANOTHER PATTERN ANOTHER PROGRAM

INSPIRES OTHERS TO CHOOSE AGAIN

LIGHT WORK

INSPIRATION

MOTHER EARTH

COLLECTIVE CONSCIOUSNESS KEEPS RECYCLING SAME PROGRAMS

FREE WILL → PRINCIPLE → THOUGHTS → MANIFESTATION

Creating the Planetary Shift

To be a Master of Manifestation also means creating the planetary shift by putting your attention on the Perfect World. You cannot do this until you effectively put your attention on Perfect Health, Prosperity, Love, etc. for yourself and all of humanity. Actually they are all one and the same.

Choosing a New Model

Step 1: Understand the mechanism (principle / how the mind works)

Step 2: Choosing a new model

Step 3: Demonstrate (Jesus did)

What does this teaching, this new model mean in practical behavior?
- Disengage from the collective consciousness.
- Don't participate in collective patterns, games. Drop out.
- Don't support the lesser. Don't give your attention to the lesser.
- Choose new models for every area of your life:
  - Your health
  - Your relationships
  - Your body
  - Your finances
  - Your beauty
  - Your business
  - You power (your hemisphere of influence)
  - Your future
  - Your past (rewrite it!)
  - Your options
  - Your view of the world
  - Your view of society
  - Your view of the Earth
  - Your view of your friends
  - Your view of your family

In short: New models for living

CHOOSING A NEW MODEL

| GOD REALIZATION | → | GOD REALIZATION | → | GOD REALIZATION |

THE STATE OF PURE BEING

BLISS ↑

↑

THE SINGLE EYE

↑

NO ANGUISH

↑

NEW MODELS → CHOOSING PEACE, LOVE
↑

TOOLS → PRAYER, MEDITATION, PRACTICING THE PRESENCE OF GOD, 7 DAY MENTAL DIET
↑ ↓

↑ ↓

MASTERS
↑

TEACHERS
↑

TEACHERS
↑

ANGUISH → OLD MODELS → COLLECTIVE CONSCIOUSNESS, CONDITIONED RESPONSES

THE STAR TRANSMITTER

The *Star* Transmitter

(This transmission was received during a group meditation in Copenhagen, Denmark on April 22, 1998. There were 6 people in the group.)

Dear Friends, this transmission is designed to teach you how to make yourselves into a "Star" transmitter for the Higher Frequencies. And to show you and guide you in ways you can use your physical bodies to become more sensitive transmitters for Divine Energies.

We call this creating a "Star"...

To create a "Star", you must become One Body.

To do this, we ask all 6 of you to lie down flat on the floor. Lie on your backs—with your heads all pointing towards the center of the circle. In the center of the circle, place a large crystal or a large rose quartz such as the one you have here. Any other type of large quartz or crystal is fine.

When you are all lying down, you will have formed a "Star". It is important that you are all lying in an open position, in other words, you arms should not be crossed on your chests but lying flat on the floor alongside your bodies. There should be nothing blocking the flow of energy from the center of the "Star" through your bodies out into the Universe.

Now it is important to relax. So please breathe deeply and gently and release all the tension in your bodies. Just relax and let go. Let us do some deep breathing together for a minute or two.

The first step in creating a "Star" transmitter is to harmonize the vibrations of the Group. Only in this way can you 6 become One Body—One "Star".

Now that everyone is relaxed, let us harmonize the breathing of the Group by chanting OM together. It is important to pick one person to lead the chanting. Everyone in the Group should breathe and chant in exact harmony with the leader. It is also important that everyone "tone" in harmony with the leader. Now let us harmonize by chanting OM together for about 3-5 minutes.

OM chanting (3-5 minutes).

That was very good. Now the Group is more harmonized.

Next I would ask each person in the "Star" to visualize their Crown Chakra opening and expanding, ever so gently. Visualize and feel the Light from the Higher Dimensions pouring down into the Center of the Circle and then radiating out from the Center and entering your Crown Chakra. Feel your Crown Chakra opening. Then feel this pulsating White Light moving down into your Third Eye Chakra and feel your Third Eye Opening. Next let this Loving, Healing Energy move down to Your Throat Chakra and feel it gently opening. Now feel your Heart Chakra opening and expanding with Love and Light. Next feel this wonderful Healing Energy moving down into your Solar Plexus Chakra and opening it. Then let this wonderful Energy continue down through your Hara Chakra and Root Chakra, opening them and healing them with Love and Light.

Now visualize that all your Chakras are open.

See the Light streaming down through your Crown Chakra—flowing gently through your entire body and streaming out from your fingertips and from the soles of your feet and toes—flowing out into the world and out into the Universe.

132

Now see and feel that you are all part of "One Star"—and see the Love and Light streaming out from the center of this "Star" in all directions. Healing Everyone and Everything that it meets on its pathway.

Now please repeat after me:

We are One Star
We are One Being

We are One Star
We are an open channel

We are now a cosmic transmitter
We are now fully functional
We are ready

We are now a transmitter for Divine Energy
We are now a transmitter for Divine Love

We are One Star
We are One Being
There is no resistance in us
We are completely open

We are an open channel for Love and Light
We are an open channel for Love and Light

We see this Love and Light flowing out in all directions
We see this Love and Light healing us as it flows through our bodies
We see this Love and Light healing all that it meets on its pathway through the Universe

Please remain with this thought in silence for the next 5 minutes. As you visualize the "Star" you have become, see your "Star" sending Love and Light in all directions. See this Love and Light healing your own bodies and everything it meets on its pathway.

(5 minutes of silence)

Very good. To be as pure a transmitter as possible, it is important to keep harmonizing the Group's energies. So let us chant OM again for a few more minutes. Everyone should focus on harmonizing with the leader's breathing so that you are all breathing in harmony. Also it is very important to chant using tones that harmonize, so please try to harmonize the sound of your voices with the sound of the leader's voice.

(OM chanting)

Very good my friends. This "Star" you have become tonight is the "Angrath Star". There is no other "Star" with exactly the same qualities as this "Star" anywhere else in the Universe. Every time you 6 join together in this way, you will become the "Angrath Star". But every Group that joins together to form a "Star" automatically becomes a special, distinct "Star" configuration with its own unique "Star" qualities. Therefore I encourage you all to join together with other friends to form different "Star" constellations. This is a very powerful way to increase the Power of Groups to do important healing work on the Planet at this time.

You will find that you can use this "Star" transmitter for many purposes. For example: Besides sending Healing Energies out into the World, a Group can ask for specific guidance when a "Star" is formed. Powerful guidance will always come when a Group is unified in asking together. The "Star" can also channel its Healing

Energy towards one person for a specific healing—or channel its Energies to heal a specific situation. It is important to trust your Guidance when you are One like this.

The more you can harmonize your energies into One "Star", the more Powerful your experience will be. When the Group is very relaxed and you all feel that everyone has surrendered their individual egos and identities as much as possible and is really experiencing the "Star" as "One Star" with One Body, you can all let yourselves go and feel yourselves spinning in a Wonderful clockwise Spiral movement through Space—and through the Dimensions. Because this is in fact the Truth about how we of the Higher Realms perceive you. When you Trust enough, you will be able to see and feel this wonderful Truth, too. And you will discover just how blissful it is... more and more Blissful...

The more you can open, the greater the Bliss...

Dear Friends, we send you Love and Light.

Evolution of Consciousness

As consciousness evolves—as a being becomes more and more conscious—he/she moves from the state of unconscious Perfection, through the stage of identifying with the personality and the form nature, to becoming a fully conscious being who again experiences Perfection. As the being progresses on the path through mind management, meditation and conscious focusing, he/she returns to the state of Pure Being, but is now fully conscious of the experience of Perfection. This evolution of consciousness is taking place in every soul.

Regardless of the stage of development, Perfection and/or the state of Pure Being, is always fully present *here now*. Beings who are trapped in the focus of their "little minds" are just unaware of It.

Enlightenment comes when the consciousness of a being is no longer identified with the mental or physical form nature—but rests in the state of Pure Being.

Evolution of Consciousness

Stage		State
Enlightened Masters Ascended Beings 5th Dimension ↑	Conscious Perfection	State of Pure Being
Post-thinking (Mind is now a tool) ↑	Conscious Perfection	State of Pure Being
Mind Management (Thinking under control) ↑	Focus on Nature of Reality	State of Pure Being (Fleeting glimpses, remembering)
Thinking (uncontrolled) ↑	Identified with the form nature Experiences good and evil, suffering, death	(State of Pure Being forgotten)
Pre-thinking (No conscious thought) (Animals, plants, nature)	Unconscious Perfection	State of Pure Being

Your Mighty I AM Presence

The evolution of consciousness proceeds like this:

1) First you identify with your thoughts and emotions. You think they are real and you think this is who I AM. (As long as you identify with your thoughts and emotions, there is suffering.)

2) Second you identify with your mind and think this is who I AM.

3) Third you identify with the witnessing consciousness and think this is who I AM.

4) Finally, when enlightenment comes, you are ABSOLUTE being.

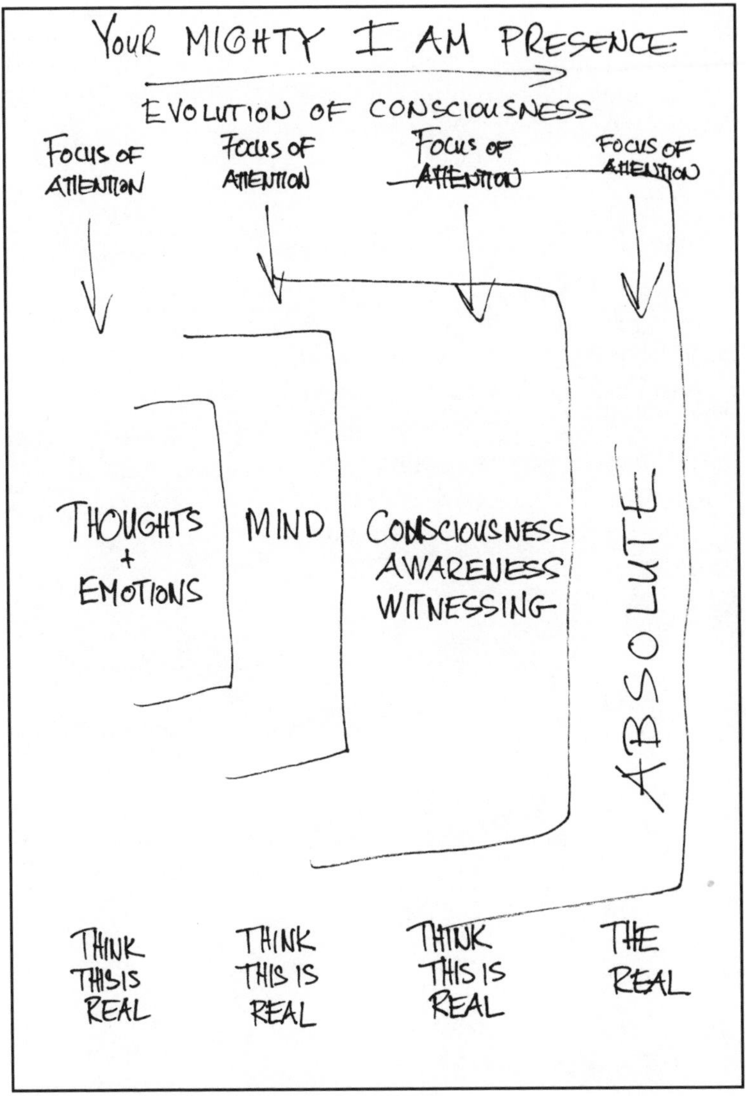
YOUR MIGHTY I AM PRESENCE
EVOLUTION OF CONSCIOUSNESS
FOCUS OF ATTENTION
FOCUS OF ATTENTION
FOCUS OF ATTENTION
FOCUS OF ATTENTION
THOUGHTS + EMOTIONS
MIND
CONSCIOUSNESS AWARENESS WITNESSING
ABSOLUTE
THINK THIS IS REAL
THINK THIS IS REAL
THINK THIS IS REAL
THE REAL

MODES OF EXPERIENCING

↑ SPIRIT = TRANSCENDENCE ↑
↑ SELF = DETACHMENT/WITNESSING
↑ MIND = ATTACHMENT   ↑

BEFORE WITNESSING =
THE PERSON MAY BE CONSCIOUS
BUT IS NOT AWARE OF BEING
CONSCIOUS,

HE/SHE IS COMPLETELY IDENTIFIED
WITH WHAT HE/SHE THINKS, FEELS,
EXPERIENCES = NOT KNOWING ONESELF

>

(THE WITNESS = KNOWING ONESELF)

Points to Remember

In fact, nobody has ever bothered you. You're just bothering yourself.

Just forget about who you think you are and it will disappear.

God is the Hassle-Free Boyfriend/Girlfriend.

Our incarnational agendas are different

The Truth is true whether you demonstrate it or not.

You just have to calm down enough to calm down.

Do not put yourself in any situation that does not feel like Love.

Where are we evolving to? What is the Highest Thought in the final analysis?
The Christ Consciousness, God Realization.

We have one thing to give, namely, our attention.

Exercise no self-scrutiny.

All this Earth experience is but Light and shadows.
Tell us what it means… What did you learn?
The only thing that matters is soul growth.
That's what your Light and shadows creations are for—for soul growth.

Take it for granted that...
...the universe supports you
...that everything is Good for you
...that Good health is your natural state
...that prosperity is your Divine right
...that you are doing great service
...that everybody loves you

Dream a better dream... it's all one big dream machine anyway.

The Perfect *Here Now*

In a perfect moment of bliss, the *Perfect here now* appears. Behind the ever changing, restless world of light and shadow is another realm, the Blessed Realm, the realm of the Absolute, the world of Infinite Goodness and Perfection. Everything there is bright and pristine clear. A white light is shining and there are no shadows at all. Everything is more beautiful, more immaculate, more clean and clear than words can describe. Thus words are only signposts, but their intent here is crystal clear—to point you in the direction of the *Perfect here now*.

Know that It does exist. Know that the time and the place are *here now*, not behind, not ahead, not tomorrow, not beyond, not anywhere but *here now*. Know that you are living in It and of It. Know that this Blessed Realm is You—your very nature. Know you are part and parcel of It, a Perfect Manifestation of a Perfection so unimaginable that you can only experience It, be It, breathe It, live It.

There is an indescribable brightness so luminous and quiet, so peaceful and free... and then you see *you have walked there always*. And your pathway left no tracks, no traces, no despair. For no disturbance exists in the Blessed Realm, only Perfection. More perfect than words can describe. And you are *perfectly at home there*, always were, always will be.

But where?

When?

Just follow the signposts, written in the fiery light of your heart—indelible in your soul. It is not difficult.

In fact, it is the easiest thing in the world. It is surrendering to your destiny, to the Goodness that has been waiting for you since the beginning of time.

Why? There is no why.

Quite simply this is the technology of you.

Soul technology.

The Perfect State of Perfect Love and Light—you know the taste even now, though long forgotten.

But the state itself is indescribable and can only be experienced.

PART TWO
MIND MANAGEMENT

Part Two: Mind Management

One of the most important aspects of soul development or evolution is mind management.

The mind is a fantastic tool, but you have to learn how to manage it properly—and to realize that your mind is *not* who you are.

Most people are unfortunately managed *by* their minds, rather than managing their minds. By this I mean, most people are driven by their random thoughts and conditioned responses and they mistake these thoughts and reactions for who they are.

The appearance generated by the sum total of these random thoughts and conditioned responses is what is called your "personality". In other words, your personality is the way in which your random thoughts and conditioned responses or reactions to events and situations define who you are.

But this appearance is not who you really are.

You are a Divine Soul, a free Spirit on an eternal journey—and you have been endowed with a fantastic tool, your mind. But to achieve the heights and glory you were destined for, you must first learn to control this wonderful tool.

This is why all the great teachers and spiritual masters teach mind control or mind management as I call it.

Without mind management, there can be no soul development.

Mastery of the mind is such an essential aspect of soul development because without it, there is no freedom. In other words, the being is not free. Proper use of free will implies the conscious ability to manage or control the mind.

Put briefly, we could say mind management means the ability to think about _what_ you want to think about—_when_ you want to think about it. It also means the ability to otherwise _be here now_ when you do not choose to think about anything specific.

There are many ways to achieve this goal of mind management.

In this section, I would like to explore some of the ways.

For more information about mind management, see my books *The Road to Power / Fast Food for the Soul* and *Mental Technology / Software for Your Hardware*.

Why Tame the Mind?

Taming the mind is so important because thought is the causative factor in the Universe.

In brief we can say the universal mind is creating all of manifest creation, i.e. the greater reality. In the same way, each human being's thoughts are determining his/her experience of manifest creation, this greater reality.

At the present time, most beings on the planet are unaware of this—and are unaware of how their minds work. They do not realize that their thoughts, in the most concrete of fashions, are creating their experience of reality. As a result, human beings often feel they are victimized by outside forces and circumstances which they believe are beyond their control instead of feeling they are able to live and experience the reality of their choice.

However unlikely this may seem, no one is being victimized.

Each being *is* in truth creating his/her own experience of reality, each and every minute of the day, whether or not he or she is aware of it.

Thus the most important realization in relation to mind management is this: *Mind is cause.* Not outside circumstances. In other words, *thoughts create our experience of reality.*

Another way of expressing this truth is: *First Mind. Second the world and all phenomena.*

For the individual this means: Your thoughts are creating your experience of reality. By thinking the thoughts you are thinking, you are choosing and creating the reality you are experiencing.

This is why taming the mind is so important.

Without the ability to manage your mind, you will always be a victim of your random thoughts and unable to achieve states of higher consciousness. States of higher consciousness are the concrete result of focusing the mind on Pure Being *here and now* and of directing mental activity to uplifting and enlightening thoughts such as Peace, Love, Compassion, Strength, and Support. To be enlightened, you have to consciously choose to think and entertain enlightened thoughts.

Observe Your Mind

When you begin to observe your mind, i.e., your thinking processes, you will quickly discover that you are thinking all the time—and that you can't just stop thinking. There is an inner dialogue going on all the time inside your head and you cannot suddenly stop it even if you want to. Unless you have been practicing meditation (quieting the mind) for a very long time, you will find that it is impossible to stop this inner dialogue no matter how hard you try.

When you realize this, the truth of the statement—*you are always thinking*—becomes apparent.

Since you are always thinking, you are always creating. You are always creating the reality you are experiencing.

So the next step in conscious mind management is to observe *what* you are thinking.

Here again it becomes quickly apparent to most people that their minds are running along like an express train that is out of control. In other words, they are not thinking about what they want to think about. Rather they are constantly thinking about all sorts of trivia—everything from what to buy at the supermarket tomorrow to the movie they saw last night and their partner's remarks in bed this morning. Very rarely does this inner chatter ever stop. It just keeps repeating itself.

If, however, enlightenment or God realization is the result of high thoughts, of enlightened or God-like thoughts, where are these thoughts? These enlightened thoughts must be *here now* and fully present in your mind—to create enlightened or God-like experiences or results. But how can you think God-like thoughts if your mind is rushing along like a freight train, thinking about everything else, including the kitchen sink? It is impossible.

Observations like this lead to the following conclusion: If you want to think enlightened, God-like thoughts, you must take control of your mind. In other words, if you are going to think enlightening thoughts, you are going to have to tell your mind to do so. It doesn't happen by itself. If you want this to happen, you are going to have to consciously manage your mind—and choose your thoughts with care.

Once the attempt has been made—to tell your mind what to think—you will discover that it is far more difficult than you imagined it would or could be. And you will begin to understand why there is an art and science to managing your mind!

Enlightenment Is not Accidental

So we see that enlightenment is not something that just happens by chance. It is not an accident—rather enlightenment is something you choose.

Of course beings may experience "moments of enlightenment" that are triggered by circumstances, events, or certain insights. And of course, these insights can be extremely powerful and transformative, but they are not the sustained, permanent state of enlightenment. True enlightenment, i.e. the permanent state of God realization—the permanent state of living *here and now* in the Eternal Present—the state of Pure Being—is a matter of choice. In other words, those beings who have attained this state of consciousness have made the conscious decision to strive for and achieve this state. Then they focused their attention on it and went to work in a dedicated manner to achieve it. Think about Buddha and the Christ. Their states of enlightenment were the result of many years of dedicated efforts on their part to understand the Nature of Reality.

So to be enlightened or God realized, how should you use your mind? What and how should you think? What thoughts are conducive to this state? What should you focus your attention on?

The Link Between Soul Technology and Mind Management

There is a definite link between soul technology and mind management. The realized soul is responsible for his or her inner space, including his/her mind. Thus effective mind management becomes one of the main tasks of beings on the Spiritual Pathway.

The evolution of mind management usually proceeds like this (see stages on the next page): First the so-called little mind—the mind that creates the person's personality—manages the person. This is the stage of unconscious thinking that most people today are experiencing. In other words, the little mind is managing their affairs for better or for worse and they are not aware of the process or of what is going on. They are unconscious. Next comes the process of becoming conscious or aware of the mind and the thinking process and how thoughts are creating one's experience of reality. When this awareness is strong enough, beings begin to try to take control of their minds and their thinking processes. In other words, a new level of consciousness is reached and the person begins to "witness" and observe the mind—and to experiment with mind management. As the ability to manage one's thoughts increases, the person starts to realize the far-reaching consequences of mind management and important life changes are initiated and achieved. The person is becoming "conscious".

If the being is then inspired to continue this evolution, the next step is often the development of a more

154

spiritual perspective. With this comes the realization that the little mind is but a focal point in the Great Mind—the ONE Mind. When the being realizes after enough study that the ONE Mind is synonymous with Perfect Good, Pure Being, Perfect Peace and Harmony *here and now*, the conscious decision can be made to surrender to the Great Mind.

The Evolution of Mind Management

1st stage: The little mind—your mind—manages you for better or for worse. (You are not conscious of this happening.)

2nd stage: You take control of your mind and begin to manage your mind—for the better. (You are now conscious of what is happening.)

3rd stage: You surrender (consciously) to the Great Mind—to the ONE Mind—and let the Great Mind manage you. (This is a conscious decision). This is the practical application of soul technology. This is what Jesus meant when he said his yoke was easy. This is true meekness. Surrender to the Divine Mind, which is unlimited Good.

In order to reach the 3rd stage, you have to constantly and consciously manage your mind.

Taming the Mind

Thus however exciting it is to know you've got this fantastic tool—your mind—which you can use to create the best possible life for yourself, if your goal is to experience states of Pure Being, you must learn to consciously direct yourself toward these states and towards enlightenment.

This means that to achieve the heights you were destined for, you must not only tame your mind—you must also learn to manage it properly.

This is possible.

Others have gone before us and have demonstrated that it is possible.

This is the example set by the Great Masters.

This is the Spiritual Pathway we are now treading.

Taming the mind is but one step along the pathway of initiation.

Resting in the state of Pure Being is further down the pathway.

But how do we get there? How do we do it?

Blissful States of Consciousness

Not only have the great Masters demonstrated for us that it is possible to find and rest in the state of Pure Being, they have shown us the way. These are the pathways we ordinary human beings can tread upon and which will take us to the blissful state of Pure Being that we so yearn for.

Resting in this blissful state is called enlightenment.

It is connecting to the Higher Self and being fully present *here now*. It is finding and connecting to that deep and profound Peace that is our true nature. All of these experiences are our true estate and birthright— the experience of Pure Being that we all seek.

Once we have experienced just a taste of this bliss, we realize that nothing can compare to the delight and peace of Pure Being.

This, our true estate and birthright, is where we came from and where we are going. This is the way we always were. This too is in fact the way we already are. And always will be. In truth we are already there, we have just forgotten. Forgotten what It is, forgotten where It is, forgotten It is *here, there, everywhere*—forgotten how to access It and connect to It, forgotten our true state and estate.

But we can remember, relearn and reconnect.

Profound Bliss

I have experienced such states of profound bliss—and this experience has totally altered my life. The bliss I have experienced is so profound that when I am there, I want to stay there always. It is like falling into a vast deep pond of sweet silence. Or entering a great immense hall that is empty, yet warm and comforting and completely safe.

It is electric and alive. Yet utterly peaceful and calm.

It is Home. Vast and deep.

It is profoundly and absolutely still.

And completely and perfectly OK.

When you surrender to this profound state of Perfect Peace you become so serene and quiet inside that you cannot imagine ever leaving It. The silence is so vast and deep and gentle that once It enfolds you, you feel utterly and completely *cared for* and *content.*

When you find this place, you know, without a shadow of a doubt, that this is your true inheritance—your true estate—Pure Being.

I have now learned how to access this place, this peace, this bliss. It has taken me some time and diligent practice, but now I know where It is and how to get there. And I am more and more able to *be* in this place, which is right *here now*. Thus this state—my true state—the state of Pure Being has become a more and more real and satisfying Presence in my life. So satisfying that I find myself spending more and more time there.

Even during my daily activities, when I am not completely there—I know where It is now and I feel Its Presence. This Presence—and my conscious awareness of the Presence of Pure Being—is almost always with me as I go about my daily business of living and working. Slowly but surely, this conscious awareness of the Presence of Pure Being is becoming a more and more real and substantial part of my daily life.

Diving into It

Ever since I discovered my true estate—the state of Pure Being—it has become more and more important for me to find time every day to dive into this state. In fact, this has become the number one priority for me—because this is where I experience bliss so profound and joy so complete, that It is far beyond my comprehension. Nothing in my life has prepared me for this experience. All I can say is that when It came, It overwhelmed me with Its grace and magic.

But no one can tell you that this is so, you have to experience It for yourself.

Since this experience is so important to me—and so satisfying—I have learned what techniques or pathways get me there the quickest. Get me to the *here now*—immediately.

But I am also realizing that in the end, I will discover that *I need do nothing at all*. IT is just there—or rather *here now*.

Pathways to Pure Being

I would like to share this information with you because most specifically you will be asking—how does one reach this blissful state of Pure Being? This blissful state of *here now*?

There are two very effective pathways—or consciousness activities—that can be used to access the blissful state of Pure Being. One pathway is what I call "no-mind meditation". The other is what I call "focusing and contemplation". But before we examine these two pathways, I would like to point out the importance of non-resistance.

Non-Resistance

Allowing yourself to become totally non-resistant makes it so much easier to access the state of Pure Being. By being non-resistant, I mean letting your so-called "critical mind and/or critical thoughts" just fall away. By being non-resistant I mean allowing yourself to be *here now*—and letting yourself be truly and totally non-judgmental. Just let all thoughts of blame drop from your mind. Release every critical thought you've ever had about anyone or anything—just let them go. At least for a while (you can always get your critical thoughts back if you want to!)

This allowing yourself to be truly non-resistant, blameless and non-judgmental is probably one of the quickest routes to the state of Pure Being around. And may be one of the Masters' best-kept secrets—or otherwise it's just so obvious that most of us don't get it.

Why does the state of no blame open the door to the *here now* state of Pure Being? Probably because by letting your mind rest in its natural state of no-blame, no resistance, no judgment, you are no longer occupying yourself with most of the energy-draining chatter that is going on in your mind during the course of the day. Often dropping critical thoughts will leave you feeling totally blank, empty—like a vast and stormy ocean that suddenly becomes quiet and calm. It's amazing.

And when you drop all thoughts of blame, criticism, accusation, condemnation and judgment, you suddenly find that you have no opinions. You are just *here now*. You are free. Free to *be.* Free to *be here now*.

This in itself is the first, delicious taste of Peace.

The other thing about this non-resistant state is that it allows the Truth, the Absolute, to come forth. Thus, the Divine Prototype, contact with your Higher Self, the Divine—which has been there all along—is made easy. With nothing to distract you, you suddenly see. And lo and behold, the True You emerges all by itself. You need do nothing except *watch and be here now*.

No Mind Meditation

The aim of "no mind meditation" is to quiet the mind and go beyond the thinking process into the Infinite *here now* and experience the state of Pure Being. Since the minds of most people are usually out of control as we discussed previously, it overwhelms them with a constant deluge of pointless random chatter. This inner mental dialogue is often so overwhelming that it prevents beings from experiencing their true state of Pure Being. Instead, people are caught in a whirl of constant mental activity—and mistake this chatter for who they are and for Life itself.

No mind meditation aims to turn off this mental chatter so the being can experience the blissful state of Pure Being *here now*. Accessing this state through no mind meditation is the traditional Eastern approach to enlightenment, also called Nirvana, Samadhi, Satori, etc. This is the experience of being *here now* Perfect and Whole. With nowhere to go and nothing to do. In the West, this experience of the Absolute reality behind the constantly changing world of phenomena is called among other things "God realization", the Christ consciousness, unity consciousness, cosmic consciousness, etc.

During no mind meditation, various techniques can be used to quiet the mind and increase present moment awareness. The most simple (and often the most difficult) is to just sit quietly and focus on the *here now*. Another is to sit quietly and focus on the breathing.

Since the mind is so powerful, this sitting quietly and focusing on the *here now* or on the breathing can be extremely difficult to do because one is constantly getting caught up in the inner mental chatter. If you are trying to use these techniques, when your inner mental chatter takes over, just gently refocus your attention on the *here now* or on your breathing.

Mantras and No Mind Meditation

Using mantras—sacred sounds or words—to quiet the mind can be very effective because repeating a mantra distracts the mind by giving it something to focus on. And while your mind is busy repeating the mantra, you can be released from its iron grip and become conscious of and experience the greater consciousness which is the real you, your true state of Pure Being, the *here now*, which is beyond your mind.

Even using a simple mantra such as OM or MA OM (MA on the in breath, OM on the out breath) can be highly effective. You can also use words like *deep peace* or *here now perfect and whole*–or a simple affirmation like *Divine Love is working in and through me*. Again just keep repeating the words silently in your head and allow yourself to calm down. When your mind starts to wander, just gently return your focus to the mantra or to the words you have chosen to repeat. Of course the repetition of certain words has a much greater impact if they are highly charged and meaningful for you. By this I mean, it is no good repeating *Divine Love is working in and through me* if you do not have some idea or some highly charged images of the qualities of Absolute, unconditional, universal Love in your consciousness. (See Love is Kind (a meditation) on page 109.)

Another powerful mantra is the ultimate statement of being: *I AM THAT I AM*. This esoteric phrase has been used throughout the ages to express in words the ultimate state of Pure Being—being without limitation. Repetition of *I AM THAT I AM* immediately connects you to the high energy frequency of the Presence, Pure Being.

162

Witnessing and No Mind Meditation

Another good way of quieting the mind is to practice "witnessing". To do this, just sit and "witness" your mind and yourself. When you do this, you will find that the moment you focus your attention on watching your mind—you can actually do it. Because you discover that there is in fact a greater Presence, a consciousness that is able to watch your mind. And who or what is this greater Presence? Obviously this Presence or consciousness must also be you. Who else could it be?

You could also say this exercise—this conscious witnessing—triggers a shift in focus from the personality focus to a soul focus. In other words by making the decision to witness your mind, you shift your attention from your little mind and your opinions to your soul or Higher Self, i.e., to the greater you that is your true state.

Thus the ability to watch or witness your little mind actually separates you from it and allows you to experience the Greater Mind, which is also the greater you. And this gives you access to the state of Pure Being since they are identical. When practicing witnessing, don't try to control your mind, rather just let your mind do whatever it wants to do and just watch it. Always gently returning to the present moment—to the *here now*—and to the witnessing Presence when you find yourself getting sucked into your mental chatter.

But as I said before, this ability to keep returning to the greater consciousness, to the state of Pure Being is not always easy to do. It is something that must be learned and it often takes diligent practice and repeated effort to master. Effort in the sense that the decision to sit and watch—and focus on the witnessing Presence must be made by you. In other words, *the choice to be conscious is a conscious choice that you must make.* But the more one practices, the easier it gets to quickly connect to that blissful state, which is Pure Being. Enlightenment comes when a being has the ability to remain connected to his or her true state—Pure Being—the eternal *here now*—all the time.

Silence and No Mind Meditation

Focusing on or listening to the silence is another way to connect to your true state of Pure Being—to the eternal *here now*. There is a deeper silence that is always present. This silence is always here with us. It is the silence of the Absolute, the silence of Pure Being. And experiencing it is pure bliss.

Most people are so distracted by the chatter going on in their own heads that they never hear this silence so they don't even know it exists or what it is. But finding it, connecting to it and listening to it, is the most blissful of experiences. It is truly diving deep.

Again, the key to experiencing this blissful silence is to make the *conscious choice* to listen to the silence. As soon as you do this, as soon as you decide to focus your attention on the silence, both within you and around you—you will discover it is there. Again, focusing on the silence will help you leave your mental chatter behind and connect to the greater consciousness. Once again this is another way of becoming aware of the Presence, of your true state of Pure Being, which is pure bliss.

Conscious Focusing and Contemplation

There are other ways to access the state of Pure Being. Conscious focusing on the Absolute and contemplation of the Divine are also excellent ways to experience the bliss of Pure Being. While "no mind" meditation is a typically Eastern approach, focusing and contemplation are more typically Western approaches. This type of practice involves a conscious, directed movement of mind and focused thinking. When practicing "conscious focusing", you make the decision to focus your attention on the nature of the Absolute, on your true state, which is Pure Being.

To do this, you set aside a specific time and place to think about the Nature of Reality. Then in your mind, you systematically go through, for example, the seven aspects of the Absolute, the ONE Mind, God, Brahma. By contemplating, the true meaning of each of the seven aspects of the Absolute—Life, Truth, Love, Intelligence, Soul, Spirit, and the Unchanging Principle of Perfect Good—you lead yourself slowly but surely into a state of pure bliss. It should, however, be noted that the prerequisite for this type of focusing and contemplation is the previous study of the Nature of Reality. If, for example, you are contemplating the seven aspects of the ONE, you must have previously studied or read about these aspects so you have a frame of reference and the appropriate images to dwell upon. When you have this frame of reference, each of these aspects can then serve as a trigger for higher states of consciousness. When dwelling like this on the various aspects, the words themselves act as signposts, creating an energetic pathway to higher consciousness. (See Appendix page 195 for an in depth description of the seven aspects or my book *Mental Technology / Software for Your Hardware*.)

Another reason why previous study is absolutely vital is that contemplation, for example, of each of the seven aspects of the Absolute is not contemplation of the dualistic qualities of the relative world, but rather of the qualities of the Absolute. Without previous study, it is almost impossible to do this.

Take the Love aspect for example. When contemplating Love, you do not dwell on thoughts of sentimental or romantic love, which is a personality-based experience, but rather on the qualities or characteristics of Divine Love. Personality-based love is an emotion that can easily swing to its opposite. It is a dualistic emotion. Divine Love, however, is true Love. It is Absolute and unconditional, i.e., it is the nature of the Absolute. Divine Love of course includes all the positive aspects of romantic or motherly love—multiplied to Infinity, in other words, without any limitation. But Divine Love is also so much more than we can conceive of since it is one of the permanent and unchanging aspects of Pure Being—it is the Nature of Reality itself.

Thus is becomes clear why a study of the Nature of Reality is a prerequisite for this type of contemplation. Because only in this way is it possible to focus on the true meaning of these words or signposts.

These words may be only signposts, but they represent the sum total of the understanding of the most highly evolved souls that ever walked the planet. And for us personally they also represent a great deal of metaphysical study on our part. Thus they contain within them a very high spiritual charge and are able to trigger higher states of consciousness.

You will discover, for example, when contemplating the metaphysical and spiritual meaning of Divine Love—the unconditional Love of the Absolute—that your thoughts are automatically led to ideas and concepts such as Unconditional Support, Perfect Harmony, a complete sense of At-Homeness, Understanding, Perfect Safety, Protection, Defense, Kindness, Compassion, the embrace of the Everlasting Arms and so forth. In other words images, which trigger the highest and most perfect associations conceivable. When this happens, contemplation becomes one of the quickest ways of accessing the blissful state of Pure Being. But make no mistake—it is a method that is often based on years of study.

Since I have been studying for years, this type of conscious focusing and contemplation quickly leads me to a state of profound bliss. But what precisely do I do—step by step—to make this type of contemplation work for me? Besides studying spiritual and metaphysical teachings on a regular basis, I *take the time and make the space* to actually perform this activity. This is absolutely necessary. If you want these experiences, you must make the conscious decision to allow yourself to experience your true state of being.

In this connection, I have found it is good to have what I call "Divine Triggers".

Divine Triggers

By Divine Triggers I mean practical steps that one can take to make it easier to quickly access the state of bliss one is seeking. Here are some good triggers:

Specific places can help trigger this experience. It can for example be a certain spot in nature or a special room where you meditate or contemplate regularly. It might even be your bed! Repeatedly going to the same place or being in the same room or space helps trigger this experience because by doing so, you create a space where there is a heightened state of energy. Every time you return, it is like opening a spiritual vortex. The bliss just comes pouring out.

For example, many people have remarked to me that the room at our center where we meditate every day and where we meditate once a week with groups of people acts as a trigger for them. They tell of the heightened energy of the space, which quickly helps them achieve a state that they find is more difficult to reach when they are on their own.

Special spots in nature can have the same effect. When you repeatedly go to the same spot, you open an energetic pathway and the heightened energy of the place helps you quickly get in state the more often you return. Also just the memory of previous blissful experiences in the same place or spot triggers the state.

Specific routines also help trigger blissful states of consciousness. For example when you are alone in the silence at home or in nature, it can help to have a specific routine to follow to get yourself in state. For some this can be reading a beloved sacred text followed by a specific meditation. For others it may be a few minutes of no-mind meditation, followed by contemplation of a certain line or passage of a sacred text or of a well-loved spiritual book. It could also be the combination of a few minutes of no-mind meditation followed by contemplation of the seven aspects of the Absolute.

There are endless combinations, but when you find a combination that works well for you, the more you repeat it, the more quickly you will find it opens an energetic pathway and triggers that blissful state of Pure Being *here now* in you.

There are also other types of Divine Triggers. For example, being with a spiritual teacher or Master is a wonderful trigger. So is meditating with like-minded seekers on the path. For some it can be performing certain highly physical activities such as extreme sports or dancing. Spending time in silence, chanting, singing, visiting sacred spots, listening to meditative music can also be Divine Triggers. As one proceeds along the spiritual pathway, one naturally discovers those activities that best trigger the blissful state of *being here now.*

Different Methods / Same Result

Both the methods described above—no mind meditation and focusing and contemplation—lead to the same state of Pure Being *here now*. And even though the approaches are different, the results are the same. So obviously, you should use whatever works best for you.

I have found that it is possible to combine no-mind meditation with focusing. As mentioned previously, I find that it works well to begin a session with 5 minutes of no-mind meditation to quiet the mind before moving on to a focusing exercise such as contemplating the seven aspects of the Absolute. For me, this combination works very well.

Another thing I have discovered is that no mind meditation is more difficult than focusing. No-mind meditation demands far more practice than focusing. Focusing is easier and quicker, because it is a movement of mind, and I find that this doesn't require so much practice. On the other hand, it requires far more previous study—as explained above.

I suggest experimenting with various combinations until you find the technique that works best for you. Practice and diligence are absolute necessities on the spiritual pathway, as is the study of metaphysical and spiritual texts.

Is Meditation Necessary?

In general, Western spiritual or metaphysical literature does not issue the same call for meditation as is found in the Eastern tradition. Jesus for one never asks his disciples to meditate, but he does call upon them to constantly "Practice the Presence". "Practicing the Presence" is an oft used phrase in Western spiritual or metaphysical literature that means to focus one's attention on God, the ONE, the Absolute. Practicing the Presence means to see the Presence of God, the Good in all people and in all situations and could be said to be the Western equivalent of meditation.

To practice seeing the Presence of the Most High Good in every person and situation, you must let High Thoughts keep running through your mind all day long like a mighty river, regardless of what you are doing. This is why I say this technique is the Western equivalent to meditation—because it requires vigilant mind management and constant practice. In other words "Practicing the Presence" is a discipline that can be just as difficult as the Eastern forms of meditation.

Just as with meditation, Practicing the Presence translates—in the long term—into the attempt to maintain a constant daily focus on the Divine, on the state of Pure Being, on the Absolute. In all situations, throughout all of one's daily activities—today and for the rest of one's Life. Gradually as one masters this practice, one sees the Presence in everyone and in all situations. This change of focus is Life transforming and opens the door to the blissful state of Pure Being.

Daily Conscious Awareness

Thus we arrive at the conclusion that it is a delusion to think that one can achieve enlightenment by meditation alone. No type of meditation—no matter how effective or how long—can replace the conscious decision to *be here now* or to "Practice the Presence" throughout the course of one's day.

The conscious choice to become more and more aware of the Presence, of the state of Pure Being, and of *being here now* is in fact the goal and purpose of meditation. And through meditation, one begins to experience these expanded states of consciousness more and more in one's daily life. But the specific meditation techniques by themselves are just that— specific consciousness activities that are designed to help us access these expanded states of consciousness, i.e., the state of Pure Being.

When we realize this, we see that meditation is only a tool or support for the real work of becoming a fully conscious being *here now*. If you can achieve this state—the state of Pure Being—without meditating, that is fine. Most people, however, need the help and support of a tool like meditation to explore consciousness and as a discipline to learn to focus their attention. But again, meditation alone is not enough. It is the minute-by-minute, hour-by-hour *conscious* focus of your attention that matters. This is the true key to enlightenment and has always been the key. The enlightened being is the being who is fully present *here now* and who is resting in the state of Pure Being. Thus we see that enlightenment is a state of consciousness—and that the key to all soul evolution and to becoming a fully conscious being is to think rightly, i.e., conscious mind management, all daylong.

When this happens, you are on your way to becoming a fully realized soul, a being who is fully present *here now* and who, un-deluded by changing forms and phenomena, rests calmly in the arms of the Absolute.

PART THREE
PEACE TECHNOLOGY

Part Three: Peace Technology

Everyone wants Peace.
Peace already exists.
Peace is the Nature of Reality—and cannot be created.
Then why don't we experience it?

There are different ways of looking at and understanding the experience we call Peace. Let us explore some of them.

Love and Peace
Love is an energy field. Just think about it and you know this is true. Love is an aura, a vibrational frequency, a very special quality or feeling, in short an energy field that is kind, gentle and supportive. Everyone naturally and automatically likes to hang out in this energy field because it is comforting, non-threatening, unconditionally supportive, and makes you feel totally at ease.

The moment there is criticism, you snap out of the field.

The moment there are conditions, you snap out of the field.

The moment there is blame, anger or fear, you snap out of the field.

You can only be in the energy field of Love when there is no criticism, no blame, no anger, no judgment, no conditions, no resentment. When any of these negative thoughts or emotions arise, instantly the energy field of Love disappears. If you say to me that you can love even when your critical mind is operating, I say to you this is not True Love. This is some type of coercion masquerading as love... True Love, Divine Love, the Love of God, is Absolute and without conditions of any kind. It just is—and it's our natural state.

Peace naturally arises in the energy field called Love.

This is because in Love there is no antagonism, no criticism, no blame and therefore no misunderstanding or conflict. (How can there be misunderstanding or conflict if there is no criticism or blame?) Thus Love is the peaceful energy field that transforms and heals everything and everyone. Love is the state of consciousness or vibrational frequency that is always kind, comforting, and supportive. It is the energy field that everyone, without exception, feels and responds to.

This energy field is a prerequisite for Peace. Peace can only exist in this energy field. In fact, this energy field *is* Peace. Thus we see that Peace and Love are the same. Identical. Synonyms.

So we may ask, if Love is an energy field that is peaceful, what triggers it? How do you enter this energy field? And how can you stay there? Once again, this is where conscious mind management comes into the picture because we can only experience what we focus our attention on. Thus to experience Peace and Love, we must focus on Peace and Love and constantly think kind, loving, and peaceful thoughts. There is no other way. Such is the law. (For a practical example of how to do this, see Love is Kind (a meditation) on page 109.)

The Nature of Reality and Peace

Another way of looking at the experience we call Peace is to explore the Nature of Reality. When we do this, we discover that Peace is in fact the Nature of Reality and already exists. (To see how we arrive at this conclusion, see my book *Mental Technology / Software for Your Hardware* for a detailed exploration of the Nature of Reality.)

Once we discover that Peace is the Nature of Reality, we realize Peace already exists and must therefore be our natural state. If this is the case, it can only mean two things. Firstly, we do not have to create Peace because it is already here. And secondly, if we are experiencing conflict in our lives and in the world around us, this must be a reflection of our innermost thinking since the Nature of Reality is already Peace—and not conflict.

We arrive at this conclusion—that conflict must be a reflection of our thinking—because we know that our experiences are the result of the focus of our attention and of our basic thoughts patterns or sponsoring thoughts about Life. Thus we must conclude that if we are not experiencing Peace in our lives, we cannot be thinking thoughts that promote peace. In other words, we cannot be thinking kind, loving, compassionate thoughts. We are not thinking thoughts that are peaceful and harmonious. Can it really be that simple? This is what the Great Ones have said all along: *As within, so without.*

177

Once we understand that we will not experience Peace in the outer until we are peaceful in the inner, we must ask ourselves...how can we bring this about? Once again we come back to the basic premise: Mind management. To experience Peace, we must consciously discipline our minds and choose the focus that creates Peace.

The State of Pure Being and Peace

Resting in the state of Pure Being is another doorway to the experience we call Peace, quite simply because this state of consciousness is Peace itself. When we rest in the *here now*, in the state of Pure Being, we are naturally at Peace. We are in fact Peace itself. How could it be otherwise? And where else could Peace be except in us *here now*?

Thus we find that when we rest in our natural state—the state of Pure Being—we are at Peace. We find that Peace is our true nature; Peace is what we are. Or you could say the natural state of Pure Being is Peace.

No matter how you put it, once you have dwelt in this blessed state for even a few minutes, you understand that this is true. Peace already exists. Peace is *here now*. And it is not especially hard to find and access. All it takes is conscious intention and conscious focus. In other words, mind management.

Mind Management and Peace

Thus we find that to experience Peace, we must learn to manage our minds. Until this happens, we will not experience Peace. This is because Peace in the outer will only arise when there is Peace in the inner. Inner

Peace as we have seen precedes outer Peace. Thus when we are peaceful, Peace will automatically appear in the world around us. Since most of us are not peaceful now, the world is reflecting our own inner conflicts back to us.

The reason why we are not automatically peaceful is obvious—most of us are not in control of our minds. Rather we are unconsciously being controlled by our minds, which are reacting haphazardly and unconsciously to the massive negative input we receive on a daily basis from the media and from people around us. None of this input promotes peace—neither inner peace nor world peace. Rather most of the input we are being bombarded with on a daily basis is pure insanity. This input appeals to the lowest common denominator in men and women and stimulates violent, angry behavior.

Until we take control of our minds, we will not be able to stop the vicious cycle of conflict, war and destruction, which is the obvious result of all the negative input, thoughts and emotions that are polluting people's minds.

To stop this vicious cycle and clean up our inner space, we must learn and practice conscious mind management on a minute-by-minute, hour-by-hour basis. Nothing else will suffice.

To experience Peace, we must learn to focus on the Truth and on the Nature of Reality. When we learn to withdraw our attention from so-called "negative" outer events and instead contemplate the Great Absolute Oneness from which we all spring, we will be peaceful. When we realize that the state of Pure Being is our True State and Home, we will be peaceful. When we understand that all men, women and children on Earth belong to ONE and the same family, the Family of Man, we will be peaceful. When we understand and experience this unity consciousness at the deepest levels of our beings, we will be peaceful. When separation thinking disappears and we feel safe and at home in the universe, we will be peaceful. When this feeling of safety becomes our reality and we know there is nothing to resist and no one to fight because we are all ONE, we will be peaceful. When these thoughts fill our consciousness and become our deepest reality, Peace—both within and without—will emerge automatically.

This state of deep and lasting Peace does not happen by accident, rather this Peace is the result of clear, conscious mind management. When there is right thinking, there is also right intention and right activity. All this leads to Peace—both on the inner and outer plane.

Mind Management Means Right Thinking
Thus Mind Management and right thinking are the most critical factors when it comes to Peace. This is because of the way our minds work and the fact that our thoughts are creating our experience of our reality—both on a personal and collective level. We know this because of the law of cause and effect.

This most fundamental of mental laws tells us that our thoughts are creating our reality and not vice versa. This principle or understanding is the basis of what is today called the "science of mind". The science of mind is a study of the way our minds work—and of how our thinking creates our experience of reality.

No one can explain why this is so, but through observation and methodical testing, people have discovered that this is the basic nature of the universe we live in—that *thought is the causative factor in the universe.* Just as scientists have discovered physical laws such as the law of gravity by observing how phenomena act, in the same way, mental laws were discovered—by observation.

Every event that takes place in the outer world must have a cause. Everything that is going on in our everyday world—including the conflicts we are experiencing today—is the result of "thought". If we are experiencing conflict and disharmony in our personal lives or between groups and nations—these events must be the result of the way we are thinking. If people and countries are at war, these conflicts must be the result of our collective thoughts. Because events do not arise out of nothing, they must have a cause. So all conflict must have a cause. This means that everything—be it an argument, an act of violence, an armed conflict—must start somewhere. And that "somewhere" is in our thoughts.

This is why it is so important to examine our thinking. Because it is here we will find the root of all conflict.

This is why mind management is so important.

Once we understand this—that our day-to-day thinking is constantly creating our reality—we have the key to creating Peace—both in our personal lives and in the world at large.

Collective Belief Patterns

Just as our individual thoughts and personal belief patterns determine our daily experiences, so the collective thoughts and belief patterns of groups and nations are determining the experiences of groups and nations.

People, groups and nations have very different views of the Nature of Reality and beliefs about this experience we call "Life". As a result, they also have very different Life experiences. But whatever these experiences are, they are the outward manifestation of their basic belief patterns and thoughts. Thus the collective thought patterns of groups and the collective consciousness of humanity as a whole are determining the experience of humanity—be it war or Peace.

Wars arise because we are not in unity consciousness. Wars arise because people are not focusing their attention on loving kindness, compassion, sympathy— and all the thoughts that make the energy field we call Love emerge. Instead, people, groups, and nations have many belief patterns that lead to conflict. Their mental focus is on separation rather than unity. In other words, there is a focus on what separates us rather than on what brings us together. These mental patterns include such thoughts as "You are different from me", "I am better than you", "I am right, you are wrong", "We are the chosen, you are the heathens," "This is mine, not yours", "If you win, I lose", "They are my friends, they are my enemies," "It's your fault, not mine", "This land is mine, not yours", "You are not my brother", etc. Unfortunately the list of such separation thoughts is very long. When groups or nations share similar negative thought patterns such as these, it is a sign that these beings are not in unity consciousness. The energy field of Love is covered by a veil.

Since our thinking is creating our experiences, this type of thinking can only lead to the experience we call conflict. Why? Because this type of thinking is accusation thinking. It puts the blame on the other fellow. It finds fault with the other fellow. It is critical and criticizing. It condemns others. It supports the opinion that one person or group's way is better than another's. It is judgmental, inflexible. This type of thinking is not compassionate. Nor does it allow each soul the freedom to develop as he or she sees fit. This type of thinking does not trust in the Good of the Universe. Instead, the focus is on fear instead of Love.

In short, this is negative thinking.

This is separation thinking.

This is seeing a frightening mixture of good and evil, instead of focusing with the Single Eye on the Absolute and seeing the ONE unchanging Good that is everywhere present in all beings.

This type of negative thinking can only lead to conflict.

Peace Through Right Thinking

Thus we see that Peace is the result of right thinking—not vice versa. We don't think rightly because we are peaceful, we are peaceful because we are thinking rightly.

What is right thinking?

Right thinking means constantly thinking correctly about our fellow human beings and this thing called Life.

Right thinking means constant mind management and the conscious decision to focus on the Nature of Reality, which is Divine Love and Perfect Peace.

Right thinking means discarding all separation thoughts in relation to our fellow human beings.

Right thinking is unity consciousness.

Right thinking is focusing on the Love that supports and brings all beings together.

Right thinking means understanding that the ONE is fully present in the many, regardless of nationality, race or religion.

Right thinking is Love, the compassionate way.

Right thinking makes the energy field called Love emerge.

Right thinking is seeing the Family of Man everywhere, in every one.

Right thinking is Loving Kindness.

Right thinking is thinking about Oneness.

Right thinking means focusing on Pure Being.

Right thinking means looking towards the ONE Great Creative Force, the ONE Absolute, the Creator of all creation, that is behind/above all of manifest creation for the Divine Solution to any seeming problem, conflict or disharmony.

Right thinking is realizing that Peace is not something we have to create—rather Peace is something that already exists.

Right thinking is understanding that Peace is what we are.

Right thinking is knowing that Peace is our nature.

Right thinking is understanding that Peace is the Nature of Reality.

Right thinking is Peace.

Peace Cannot Be Legislated

Thus we see why all humanity's attempts to create world peace by legislating external conditions have so far failed. The external world is only a reflection of our inner world, both on a personal and collective level. Thus all political initiatives, no matter how well intentioned, are doomed to fail. First when each individual being gets the inside right, will outside conditions adjust themselves and Peace—our natural state—emerge.

Right Thinking Is Peace

Right thinking means:
>Focusing on the Nature of Reality
>Focusing on the state of Pure Being
>Focusing on the *here now*
>Focusing on Unity consciousness
>Focusing on Love / Loving Kindness
>Focusing on the Brotherhood of Man

Right thinking leads to:
>Right vision (A New Vision for mankind)

Right vision leads to:
>Right choices

Right choices lead to:
>Right activity
>Right relationships
>Right work
>Right politics
>Right relations to the environment

Right choices lead to Peace.

We won't experience Peace until we are enlightened.

We won't have Peace in the outer until we are enlightened.

Peace / the Perfect *Here Now*

Thus we see that Peace arises automatically when there is an alignment of one's consciousness with the Nature of Reality. This is because the Nature of Reality is synonymous with Divine Love and Perfect Peace, which are the Highest Good. When this alignment takes place, all there is… is Peace. Love. Perfect Good.

Because as we said before—as on the inner plane, so on the outer plane.

Thus when our collective thoughts are focused on Pure Being, loving kindness, unity consciousness, the Perfect *here now,* our collective reality will also be Peace—because our collective thoughts are creating our collective reality.

When we rest in Pure Being, we are Peace.
When we are enlightened, we are Peace.

Resting in Pure Being, we experience Peace.

APPENDIX

The Daily Program

In order to keep your mind flowing like a mighty river, you need signposts along the way. That's exactly the purpose of your daily program. You could say the activities in your daily program are like the stopping points during your day where you observe yourself, remind yourself, adjust your focus (or regain your focus) and raise your energy.

In the end of course, your whole life becomes one long meditation—one long praiseful symphony of song of/to/for/about all of Creation. But until then, you will probably need the signposts/stopping points of your daily program to keep you on track.

In the old days, people dedicated to the spiritual pathway often lived in monasteries—away from the so-called "everyday" world—so as not to be diverted/distracted from the spiritual pathway. Today, people all over the world are learning how to integrate a so-called "spiritual" focus in their everyday lives. And the result is as it should be—a greater sense of "here now" peace and harmony.

It is wise to set certain times during the day to stop up. For a normal day it could be as follows:

Morning: 10-20 minutes or longer
    It could be:
    Affirmations (they could be said aloud)
    Meditation / contemplation / sitting in silence

Noon: 10-15 minutes or longer
It could be (during your lunch break):
Observing silence / going for a walk in the park
Affirmations / writing affirmations in your journal
Short treatment for harmony for whatever is happening in your day

Evening: 20-30 minutes or longer
It could be:
Meditation / Contemplation
Treatment
Reading / studying (see suggested authors below)

If the above is a regular workday, you might want to have one special day or afternoon (evening) a week where you can devote yourself to longer periods of practice and reading.

Suggested Reading:
The 5 E Masters:
Eckhart Tolle
Emma Curtis Hopkins
Emmet Fox
Ernest Holmes
Eric Klein
As well as: Byron Katie, Catherine Ponder, Stuart Wilde, Florence Shovel Shinn, Deepak Chopra, Louise Hay, James Twyman, Eileen Caddy, Peter Caddy, Tim Ray, James Redfield, Neale Donald Walsch, Dannion Brinkley, Charles Fillmore, Emile

Cady, Mary Baker Eddy, the Dalai Lama, Paramahansa Yogananda, Sri Nisargadatta Maharaj, Gandhi, Alice Bailey, the Bhagavad Gita, the Bible and other sacred texts.

In general, spend more time reading and studying spiritual texts.

Food: Eat food that makes you feel light and energetic. Lots of fresh vegetables. Good bread. Grains. Less meat, sugar, processed foods. Less junk food. Less alcohol.

In general, eat less.

Exercise: The 5 Tibetan rites, Ashtanga Yoga, Yoga, fitness workouts, jogging, stretching, dancing, swimming, biking, sports activities. As a minimum, it is a good idea to exercise at least every other day for at least ½ hour. Exercising every day is better.

In general, move your body more.

Time in nature: If you live in the city, it is important to keep in contact with nature. At least once a week, spend some time in nature, preferably not talking all the time! Allow yourself to dwell on the wonder of creation.

In general, spend more time in nature.

Service: At least once a week, do something for others. As we grow spiritually we come to see that we are all one family, so it is only natural to want to contribute and do something positive, loving, kind, helpful for others. Also dedicating some time to service is one of the best ways to get the right perspective in relation to your own problems and challenges. Do something definite and concrete at least once a week to help someone else. And during the course of your day, act naturally and spontaneously from the goodness of your heart when the opportunity to assist other people arises.

In general, spend more time helping others.

A Sample Treatment

Here is an example of how to Speak the Word and "give a treatment" for yourself or for anyone else. You can use this treatment for all types of situations and problems in the seeming such as a health problem or some kind of lack or disharmony.

Just put in your name or the name of the person you are treating for in the blank spaces. Say this treatment aloud if you can, otherwise say it slowly in your head as you think deeply about the meaning of each sentence. Do this several times a day until the problem or situation clears up and Perfect Harmony is restored

"This treatment is for _____. The words that I speak are the Truth about _____ and they go forth into the Great Universal Mind and they do not return unto me void but they accomplish the things of which I speak, with mathematical precision.

There is only ONE Life and that Life is God and that Life is Perfect and that Life is _____ 's Life now. And I know that this Perfect Life is God within _____. I also know that God within _____ is stronger than anything... stronger than any difficulty... that _____ has to meet including this problem or situation with (name the problem or situation). God has given _____ dominion over my/his/her circumstances and that means that God has given _____ dominion over this problem / situation (name the problem, situation). Therefore _____ lets nothing in this situation frighten me/him/her because _____ knows that God is with _____.

I also remember what the beautiful Jesus said: "What things soever ye desire, when ye pray, believe that ye receive them, and ye shall have them" (Mark 11:24). Therefore I have Perfect Faith, the Faith of the beautiful Jesus, that what _____ needs God has already provided. And that _____ is now uncovering the Good that already exists for me/him/her in the Mind of God. I give thanks in Perfect Faith for _____ (name the Good, for example Perfect Health or Perfect Harmony) even if _____ does not yet see it with the eyes of flesh. I see the Truth, the Perfect Good, the Perfect Being, the Perfect Health, the Perfect Condition, the Perfect Harmony!

Thank You Father for I know that Thou hearest me always!

Amen.

Hallelujah!"

(For more examples of treatments, see my books *The Road to Power / Fast Food for the Soul* and *Mental Technology / Software for your Hardware*.)

Aspects of the ONE

Here are some suggestions of how to contemplate the seven main aspects of the ONE, the Absolute.

Life: Life is existence. Life is all there is. There is only ONE Life and that Life is everywhere, in everything. This ONE Life or God is the animating Force behind the entire manifest creation. This ONE Life is the First Cause—the cause of all creation. And since this Life is all there is, it means there is no opposing Force. In other words, there is nothing else in existence besides this ONE Life. This means that the ONE Life must be all-powerful and all-present.

This Life is also the very same Life that created you and that is animating you right now. The very same Life that is animating every aspect of your being. In this connection, you can focus your attention on images that bring to mind a feeling of the true power and strength of this ONE omnipresent, omnipotent Life. You can dwell on the fact that this ONE Life, with all its incredible and infinite strength and vitality, is animating you right now. This ONE Life is the very essence of your being. This is what you are. This is your true nature. Whatever is true of this ONE Life must also be true of you since this ONE Life created you and is sustaining you at this very moment.

Truth: Truth is what is. Truth is that which never changes. So the ONE Life or existence must be the Truth because the ONE Life is all there is. In fact, Life or existence is the only thing we know for sure. We know that Life is because we exist. In other words, you know that Life is because you exist. You could say that you are proof of your own existence. So this must be Truth. Ergo you are Truth.

Love: The ONE animating Force of the Universe and of the entire manifest creation has created Life and given us everything. All of Life. And this ONE Life or God is sustaining and supporting all of creation— including all of us. This means you and me. This must be Love. We could say that Love is the "givingness" of the ONE Life of itself to itself. Other words we can use to describe the "givingness" of Life are support, defense, protection and care—all of which equal Love. And since all human beings are a part of this closed loop called Life, this Love must be the very essence of our nature.

Intelligence: The dazzling, incomprehensible dance of creation is beyond our wildest fantasy or dream. The vastness of space with its myriad galaxies, the intricacies of our own bodies, the breathtaking web of all Life that extends from dimension to dimension—all of this we sense and apprehend as the Greater Life of which we all are a part. All of this, all of this vast creation is existing within the mind of the ONE, which is also coordinating and organizing this incredible dance of creation with effortless ease. This demonstrates and is proof of the all-knowing intelligence of the ONE Life.

Next consider that this is the very same intelligence that has created and is now animating you. And since you also know that cause and effect are equal and identical, you can deduce that this intelligence is also your intelligence.

Soul: The soul of man is a spark of God, of the ONE Life. God or the ONE Life has individualized itself in each one of us. And as every drop of water in the ocean carries with it the essence of the ocean, so the ONE Life is individualized but undivided in each of us. This

196

means that all of God or the ONE Life is in every bit of its creation. Thus all of this ONE animating Life force is in each one of us. Each one of us has full access to all of God. It also means that everything that is true about God or the ONE Life is true about each one of us. (A very good thing to meditate upon.)

Spirit: Spirit is another word for the ONE Life force that animates all of creation. And since we know that creation has no beginning or end, the Spirit that animates all of creation also has no beginning or end. This means that Spirit is eternal and immortal. This Spirit is the same Spirit that is animating you. So you must partake of the nature of Spirit, in other words, you too must be eternal and immortal. In this connection, you can ask yourself: Can you remember a time when you did not exist? Can you remember a time before you were born?

Principle: Since principle or law is something that does not change, the ONE Life or God that is eternal and immortal, must be unchanging principle or law. And since ONE Life is all that exists, we can deduce that this ONE Life or God is not only principle—It must be the *unchanging* Principle of Perfect Good. Why is this so? Why is the ONE Life or God the *unchanging* Principle of Perfect Good? Well think about it. What is your definition of *Good*? What is Good? Your definition, your highest definition of Good, is the same as everyone else's highest definition of Good. Good is unlimited Life—Life without beginning or end, Life that is immortal and eternal and filled with unlimited Love, Love that is unconditional and without beginning or end, which means a life of unlimited Peace and Harmony with unlimited Intelligence filled with and surrounded by unlimited Abundance. And, as we have just seen, all of these definitions of Good are the characteristics of the ONE Life, of God, the Absolute. Therefore we can deduce that the ONE Life, God, the Absolute, must be the unchanging Principle of Perfect Good.

"Locking on Target": The Exercise

This exercise has three parts:

> Grounding the Higher Self
> Contemplating the Higher Self
> Affirming the Higher Self

Part One: Grounding the Higher Self

Sit in a in a good chair with enough support so that your back is straight. Breathe deeply and relax. Begin the exercise by focusing on your breathing for a few moments or minutes. Just quietly watch your breath go in and out.

When you have settled down, you are ready to begin to visualize and work symbolically. Start by locating the 8th chakra—the point above your head where your Higher Self is located symbolically. It is easy to find this point and you won't be in doubt when you do. It is usually about 1-2 meters above your head. When you have found it, lock your attention onto it. This is what I mean by "locking on target". You will probably feel that the energy of this spot is very special, like a star or a very intense ocean of whiteness. Remember, your Higher Self is the Divine Prototype of you, the Perfect You.

Once you have locked onto this energy, bring the energy firmly but gently down to your physical body. In other words, bring the energy of your Higher Self down to the top of your head and open your Crown chakra to accept the energy of your Higher Self. What you are really doing is opening yourself to yourself! You will probably feel the top of your head tingling as you open your Crown chakra. And since you are the master, you can open this powerful energy vortex as much or as little as feels right to you. The Crown chakra is like a vast spiral galaxy that you are opening to the Infinite Intelligence of the Universe and of your Higher Self. That is why we symbolically say this is the gateway to Divine Wisdom or the Christ Consciousness.

Next bring the energy of your Higher Self down to your Third Eye chakra, which is located inside your head, between your eyebrows. Allow your Third Eye chakra to open to the energy of your Higher Self—the Divine Prototype of you. Again you can open this chakra as much or as little as feels right to you. When you focus your attention on the Third Eye chakra, you may "see" bright flashes of Light or a pulsing Light— but this is not something you see with your physical eyes. No, you are seeing the Light with your inner "Sight" because this chakra has to do with our ability to "see". Not seeing with your physical eyes, but rather seeing with the inner Sight. This is the True Visioning—the Divine Sight. (In this connection, it is important for those who are very sensitive to refuse to look at the astral or psychic plane. Affirm that your Divine sight is only open to the Light, the higher energies, and the vision of the Divine.)

Next bring the energy of your Higher Self down to your Throat chakra and allow your Throat chakra to relax and open. Release any tension in this area—and again, you may allow this powerful energy vortex to open as much or as little as feels right to you. As you open your Throat chakra to the energy of your Higher Self, you are opening yourself to the Wisdom of your Higher Self in the communications center of your body. When there is balance and harmony between your Highest Wisdom and the Love from your Heart chakra, the words that you speak will always be the right words at the right time. Words that create balance and harmony, words that bring forth the Highest Good. Remember "And the Word was made flesh..." (John 1:14). Our words are our magic wand of creation here on this Earth.

Now bring the energy of your Higher Self down to your Heart chakra and open your heart to the energy of the True You, which is in its essence Divine Love. Divine Love is who you are, is what we all are, and the opening of the Heart chakra is a most blissful experience. Allow your whole chest area to relax and feel how your breathing gets deeper and more relaxed. Breathe deeply and easily. If there is any tension around your heart, just release it. If you feel there are clouds of negativity around your heart (from hurt feelings, old emotional wounds, bad memories, negative thoughts about yourself), just say to yourself gently but firmly, "I now choose to release this energy and let it go. It is nothing to me—just an illusion I now choose to let go. I send this energy back to the Nothingness from which it came." Then focus on the Divinity of Love, which is your true nature.

(For more information, exercises and meditations to understand, feel and experience the Divinity of Love in your heart, see my book *Gateway to Grace*.)

Next bring the energy of your Higher Self down to your Solar Plexus chakra. Again feel this area of your body opening and relaxing. If you feel any tension in this area, just relax and release the tension. You can open this chakra as much or as little as feels right to you. This chakra has to do with your ability to be active here on the Earth plane, to interact with others, to do your work and be of service in the world. It is important to "ground" the energy of your Higher Self in the three lower chakras because this grounds, materializes and manifests the higher energies in your physical vehicle. If you are in doubt about this, just remember you would not have incarnated in a physical body if you were not meant to "act" in this world. By bringing down the higher energies and by grounding the wisdom of your Higher Self in the physical, your activities will become more and more balanced, harmonious and powerful as they are increasingly guided by Highest Wisdom. So breathe all the way down to this area and really bring the energy down so you feel yourself becoming heavier and more grounded.

Then move the energy of your Higher Self down to your Sacral chakra or Hara center, located about 5-6 cm below the navel. Again open and relax in this area and breathe all the way down to below your navel. As you bring the higher energies down, you will feel yourself becoming heavier and more grounded. When you ground yourself like this you will be stabilizing your being and your activities on the Earth plane and it will be more difficult for outer events, circumstances, or people to knock you out of balance or destabilize you. You will be grounded in your own inner knowledge and knowingness of who you are. And you will carry this new sense of stability and knowingness with you throughout your day.

Finally, bring the energy of your Higher Self down into the Root chakra at the base of your spine. Connect the higher energies to your Root chakra and let the higher energies go all the way down into the ground below you. Feel that you are literally connecting the highest in you to the physical here and now. That you, Spirit, your Higher Self, is literally incarnating on Earth. Then let the energy go straight down into the ground and also pass down through your legs and feet down into the Earth like deep roots, anchoring your Higher Self in the here, now.

Now truly feel how you have "grounded" the energy of your Higher Self. Understand and feel that the Divine Prototype of you is really here now, a real and tangible force that is now flowing through all your chakras, which are now open and relaxed. If you still feel tightness or tension in any of the chakra areas, you may want to chant "OM" aloud for a few minutes. Chanting "OM" really looses up the channel. As you chant, you can allow the vibratory quality of your voice to flow up and down the channel of your chakras, or you can direct the energy to a specific chakra if you feel there is a blockage or tightness in a specific area.

When you are done, you should feel very grounded, but if at any time you feel the energy rising back up to your head, you can just bring it down again from the 8th chakra to the Crown chakra, to your Third Eye chakra to your Throat chakra to your Heart chakra to your Solar Plexus chakra to your Hara chakra and finally down to your Root chakra and into the ground. Now you should feel very grounded and whole, almost as if you are sitting on your energy—because you have now fully grounded and aligned your Higher Self with your physical body.

Part Two: Contemplating the Higher Self
Now that you have grounded the energy of your Higher Self, you can use this opportunity to

contemplate who you really are. Since you are now fully connected to your Higher Self, the Divine Prototype of you, what does this mean? Who are you in Truth? And what are the ramifications of this discovery?

Since your Higher Self is the Perfect You, you can start by asking yourself what is the Perfect You like? What is the Divine You like? In other words, what is the Highest and Best version of you, you can conceive of? The Perfect You. The Divine Prototype of you. You as you have been from the beginning, from before your birth, from before the foundation of the world. Who and what is this? The Real You?

Allow yourself to envision, see, feel and enjoy the most Beautiful version of You you can conceive of. The Wisest version of You. The Most Loving version of You. The Most Enlightened, Kind, Compassionate version of yourself you can imagine. What do you look and feel like? Allow yourself to explore the possibility of the Divinity that is in you and that *is* you, because this is Who You are in Truth and this is Who you have always been and where you are going—from the very Beginning until the End of the End.

Allow your consciousness to expand with the thought of the Divine Prototype of You. Allow this energy to wash over you and bless you with its infinite Love and kindness. Allow yourself to grow into it—and Be IT— be your True Self as you have been from the Beginning.

If you still feel any tightness, tension or dark clouds of negativity in any of the chakra areas, you can chant "OM" again to loosen the clouds or you can just gently say to yourself: "I now release these clouds, these illusions of negativity from my energy field and send them back into the Nothingness from which they came. I now allow the Divine Prototype, my Higher Self, to manifest itself fully and freely in and through me."

You can also see in your mind's eye the manifestation of the Divine energy of each chakra now working in and through you. In other words, you can see and feel yourself embodying:

- Divine Wisdom or the Christ Consciousness through your Crown Chakra,
- Divine Sight, the True Visioning, and the power of the Single Eye through your 3rd Eye Chakra,
- Divine Expression, Perfect Communication and Manifestation via your Throat Chakra,
- Divine Love and the Harmonizing Factor through your Heart Chakra,
- Divine Power and Activity through your Solar Plexus Chakra
- Divine Balance and the Grounding of the Soul in this dimension through your Hara Chakra,
- And finally, embodying the Divine Physicality or Body as Spirit incarnating on Earth in the 3rd dimension through your Root Chakra.

Part Three: Affirming the Reality of Your Higher Self

Now that you have grounded and contemplated the energy of Your Higher Self, you can finish this exercise by affirming (preferably aloud) that you are manifesting the full and perfect energy of your Higher Self here and now in every aspect of your daily life.

The affirmation in my son Tim Ray's book *Starbrow – A Spiritual Adventure* is excellent for this purpose. In the original version in his book, he uses the word the "Force" instead of the "Higher Self" as I do below. But Tim and I discovered at our group meditations that this affirmation can be used just as effectively and powerfully with other words instead of the Force. For example, we found that you can substitute Love or Divine Love or Peace or the Good or Divine Intelligence instead of the Force and each time it becomes a very powerful affirmation or treatment. But for Grounding the Higher Self, using the term the Higher Self instead of the Force makes this an excellent way to end the exercise. So here it is:

"In the Beginning: My Higher Self
Here and Now: My Higher Self
At the End of the End: My Higher Self
Here, There, Everywhere: My Higher Self
From Alpha to Omega: My Higher Self
In Heaven, Upon Earth: My Higher Self
In the Greatest, in the Smallest: The Higher Self
In Fire, in Water, in Earth, in Air: The Higher Self
In Me, in You, in Everyone: The Higher Self
Above Me, Below Me, Around Me: My Higher Self
In Me, Through Me, From Me: My Higher Self
In My Thoughts, in My Words, in My Actions:
My Higher Self
My Higher Self is All in All
All Life, All Intelligence, All Love
My Higher Self is the One and Only Reality
And so it is!"

Monks Without Robes

The disciplined activities described in this book—designed to help you access the state of Pure Being—are in fact just the kind of disciplined activities that monks practice in monasteries. In these protected environments, there are highly disciplined daily practices that are designed to help the evolving beings reach higher and higher states of consciousness.

Now we find that so-called "ordinary" people like you and I, people who are living "in" the world—secular people—are beginning to practice these types of techniques on a regular basis. This is one of the great changes that are taking place in the world evolution. The spiritual practice, that was once only for the select few, is now being practiced by people who are living "in" the world. In other words, today it is no longer necessary to live in special, secluded and protected "spiritual" environments to practice these activities.

One of the reasons this is happening today is that the necessary information is now available. Books and teachings are available today on a global scale that previously only a select few had access to. So today you no longer need be a monk to have access to this information.

Of course now the challenge is how do we combine these practices with so-called "ordinary" life? In other words, how do we live like monks without robes!